From Hofie, Oct. 2014 "Eleri's Mts."

WYOMING'S
WIND RIVER RANGE

NUMBER TWO

WYOMING
GEOGRAPHIC SERIES

AMERICAN GEOGRAPHIC PUBLISHING
WILLIAM A. CORDINGLEY, CHAIRMAN
RICK GRAETZ, PUBLISHER
MARK THOMPSON, DIRECTOR OF PUBLICATIONS
BARBARA FIFER, ASSISTANT BOOK EDITOR

This series provides in-depth information about Wyoming's
geographical, natural history, historical and cultural subjects.
Design by Len Visual Design; Linda Collins, graphic artist. Printed in
Hong Kong by Nordica International Ltd.

ISBN 0-938314-54-8

published by
American Geographic Publishing
P.O. Box 5630
Helena, Montana 59604
(406) 443-2842

DEDICATION

To everyone I've traveled
with in the Wind Rivers—
those I've shared good
times with and who have
helped me see things more
clearly.

**Library of Congress
Cataloging in Publication Data**

Kelsey, Joe, 1938-
    Wyoming's Wind River range /
by Joe Kelsey.
        p.   cm. -- (Wyoming geo-
graphic series ; no. 2)
    ISBN 0-938314-54-8 (pbk.) :
$14.95
    1. Natural history--Wyoming--
Wind River Range.   2. Mountain
ecology--Wyoming--Wind River
Range.   3. Wind River Range
(Wyo.)
I. Title.   II. Series.
QH105.W8K45   1988
508.787'6--dc19   88-19824
                                CIP

CONTENTS

Front cover photo: *Alpine sunflowers, Cirque of the Towers.* JEFF GNASS
Page 1: *East Temple (left) and Temple (center) peaks, seen from the Jackass Pass Trail above North Lake.* JEFF GNASS
Facing page: *In the Popo Agie Primitive Area.* PAT O'HARA
This page, clockwise from left: *Lodgepole pine branch.* PAT O'HARA *The Wind River Mountains include sources of the three main river systems: the Colorado, Columbia, and Missouri/Mississippi.* BARBARA & MICHAEL PFLAUM *Rivers that flow from the mountains of northwest Wyoming are refuges for the rare bald eagle.* KENNAN WARD *New snow, Englemann spruce, Togwotee Pass.* JEFF GNASS

3

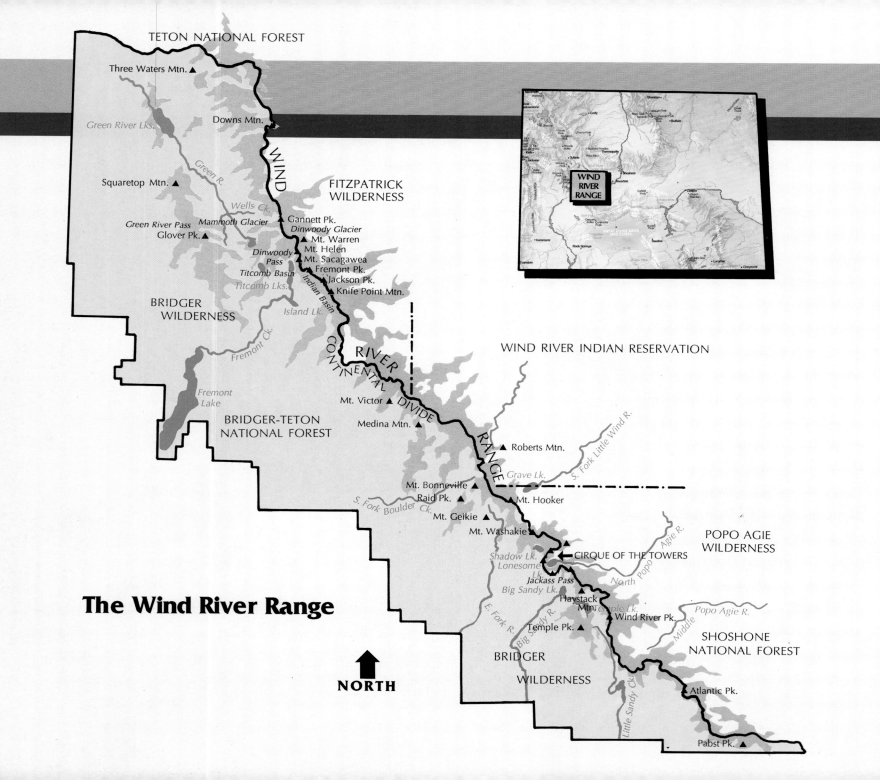

The Wind River Range

TETON NATIONAL FOREST

Three Waters Mtn. ▲

Downs Mtn.

Green River Lks.

WIND

Green R.

Squaretop Mtn. ▲

Wells Ck.

FITZPATRICK WILDERNESS

Green River Pass

Mammoth Glacier

Gannett Pk. ▲

Glover Pk. ▲

Dinwoody Glacier

Mt. Warren ▲

Dinwoody Pass

Mt. Helen ▲

Titcomb Basin

Mt. Sacagawea ▲

Titcomb Lks.

Fremont Pk. ▲

Jackson Pk. ▲

BRIDGER WILDERNESS

Island Lk.

Knife Point Mtn. ▲

Indian Basin

Fremont Ck.

RIVER

CONTINENTAL DIVIDE

WIND RIVER INDIAN RESERVATION

Fremont Lake

BRIDGER-TETON NATIONAL FOREST

Mt. Victor ▲

Medina Mtn. ▲

RANGE

▲ Roberts Mtn.

S. Fork Little Wind R.

Grave Lk.

Mt. Bonneville ▲

Raid Pk. ▲

S. Fork Boulder Ck.

▲ Mt. Hooker

Mt. Geikie ▲

Mt. Washakie ▲

▲

Popo Agie R.

POPO AGIE WILDERNESS

Shadow Lk.

←CIRQUE OF THE TOWERS

Lonesome Lk.

Jackass Pass

North Popo Agie R.

Big Sandy Lk.

Popo Agie R.

Haystack Mtn.

Temple Lk.

E. Fork R.

Temple Pk. ▲

Wind River Pk. ▲

Middle Popo Agie R.

SHOSHONE NATIONAL FOREST

Sandy R.

Big Sandy R.

BRIDGER WILDERNESS

↑
NORTH

Atlantic Pk. ▲

Little Sandy Ck.

Pabst Pk. ▲

WIND RIVER RANGE

PREFACE

I came to the Wind Rivers in a roundabout way. Hiking in New Hampshire as a kid led to rock climbing in New York, which led to visits, during the 1960s, to the Tetons, the Sierra Nevada, the Cascades, the Canadian Rockies. Around campfires, though, there was talk of lesser-known, more-mysterious mountains, whose attraction was less obvious. At first the mystery was a rock massif being named for flowing water named for moving air. But as I continued to listen the mysterious allure became this: Everywhere I had climbed we marched into the mountains purposefully—to climb routes, chosen in advance, as frequently as our schedule and the weather allowed; we measured success by the number of our objectives we achieved. From what I heard in campfire talk, life in the Wind Rivers was less purposeful. While veterans spoke highly of the rock climbing, simply being there was enough to make a climber—or hiker or fisherman—happy.

Finally, in 1969, friends invited me to join them for a week in a part of the range with a name as simultaneously misty and alluring as Cibola, Shangri La or Middle Earth: the Cirque of the Towers. One August afternoon, teetering in the wind under an absurdly heavy pack, I descended from Jackass Pass and wrestled my burden to the boulder- and flower-studded meadow by Lonesome Lake.

The next day, while less acclimatized comrades recovered from the hike, I set out alone for Camel's Hump, at 12,537' one of the higher Cirque peaks but one climbable by easy ledges. I made two discoveries: the pleasure of nontechnical climbing past tundra-like slopes, tumbling creeks and granite slabs; and the extent of the Wind River Mountains. I had heard of the highest peaks—Gannett, Frémont—which I could see 30 miles to the north, but not the nearer sea of summits whose unfamiliar names I found on a map—Washakie, Bonneville, Hooker and Musembeah; Haystack and Temple.

The next day it was back to technical climbing—the East Ridge of Wolf's Head, possibly the only rock climb to require a sense of humor, as you balance along a ridiculously narrow crest, then weave around, through and over a series of individualistic pinnacles. We climbed Pingora by its South Ridge, as clean, direct and continuously interesting a short rock climb as the mountains can offer. Pingora, with its truncated top, is no Matterhorn, is lower than its neighbors, and is invisible from civilization; nevertheless I have come to think of it as the quintessential Wind River peak and take newcomers up it for their first Wind River route. Finally, we climbed Warbonnet by its Northeast Face.

Food ran out, some friends left. But others arrived, and I went out for food and rejoined them. These friends were not climbers, and it was with them I discovered the meadows and lakes that we had inattentively crossed en route to steep rock.

Since 1969, I have spent several weeks each summer in the Wind Rivers, trips lasting from two days (not a good idea) to two weeks, typically about a week. I have made a point of exploring different parts of the range, though I frequently return to the Cirque of the Towers. I have hiked into the mountains with various motives—to get into shape at the beginning of summer, to relax at the end of summer, to try difficult climbs, to try to learn to key flowers. The weather has more often than not allowed us to do what we had planned, but I have been caught by snow every September that I can remember.

September snow dusts the Cirque of the Towers. In this view north from Warbonnet, the prominent peak in the right foreground is Pingora; to its left and slightly more distant is Wolf's Head. On the skyline, 30 miles away, are Frémont Peak and snow-capped Gannett Peak. Just left of Frémont, in the middle distance, is Mt. Bonneville. JOE KELSEY

5

ORIENTATION

Above: *Moon and lodgepole pine.*
PAT O'HARA

Right: *Warbonnet (at left) was named by early Cirque of the Towers climbers for the "feathers" on its right-hand ridge. The Warriors, also reflecting early-morning sun in Lonesome Lake, were named because of their association with Warbonnet.*
JEFF GNASS

A photomosaic of Wyoming—a composite aerial photograph—shows most of the main geographic features aligned either north-south or east-west, which seems appropriate for a state that itself is a giant rectangle. A color-enhanced photomosaic also reveals a concentration of mountains along the northern border—the Absarokas, the Bighorns—and down the western edge—the Tetons, the Wyoming Range—while across much of the eastern and southern part of the state extend the Great Plains. A mountain chain that runs diagonally, southeasterly from the alpine country of northwestern Wyoming,and bisects the arid plains, stands out, metaphorically as in reality, in bold relief.

Color enhancement further accentuates a physiographic feature of this range, the Wind River Mountains, that tells much about its scenery, climate and ecology: the white stripe indicating the range's backbone is separated from the tawny expanses of the basins to either side by a ring of dark green—a sign of vegetation, precipitation, wildlife habitat. Less obviously, the green band is a clue to the Wind Rivers' relation to humanity—their obscurity compared, say, to the Tetons, their remoteness of access, but also an ease of travel through the mountains and a feeling visitors get of being where they are meant to be.

The slant of the range's axis from northwest to southeast makes directions more cumbersome than in a north-south range. Wind River travelers have solved this problem by verbally pivoting the axis, so that northwest is "north," southeast is "south." The character of the terrain reinforces this reorientation—the one end high, covered with extensive glaciers and tundra-like, arctic plateaus; the other end a bit lower, drier, blending with the high plains of sagebrush and other desert vegetation. Snow-and-ice climbers head to the northern Wind Rivers, rock climbers to the southern Wind Rivers. To further encourage the shorthand compass, the range's northeast slope drains to the Atlantic, most of the southwest slope to the Pacific.

Flowing waters

If you imagine the Continental Divide as an entity both substantive and flowing, rather than the geographical abstraction it is, picture it entering the northwest corner of

Wyoming, via the Idaho-Montana border. Continuing southeast through Yellowstone Park, the Divide separates the headwaters of the Snake River—and thus the Columbia and the Pacific—from the headwaters of the Yellowstone River—and thus the Missouri, Mississippi and Atlantic. The Divide then cuts through the Absaroka Range to Togwotee Pass, which also separates Jackson Hole from the head of the Wind River Valley. Togwotee Pass is by definition the northern end of the Wind River Mountains.

Near the north end of the Wind Rivers gentle slopes strewn with rock rubble converge at an 11,680′ summit. Despite this massive mound's unprepossessing appearance, its lack of appeal to photographers or mountaineers, it was for a century named Triple Divide Peak and for the past decade has been Three Waters Mountain. In theory, a raindrop spattering on a certain rock near the summit (more realistically, a snowpatch melting in the spring thaw) sends droplets to the three main river systems of the west—the

The Green River originates in glaciers under the high peaks, flows down a dèep canyon past Squaretop (right of center), and below the Green River Lakes (hidden behind the wooded moraine) emerges from the mountains flowing northwest in a broad, marshy valley. ROB OUTLAW

The Green River, after turning south, flows through high desert to join the Colorado in Utah's canyonlands. From LaBarge, on the Green, the Wind River crest is visible 50 miles to the northeast. CHARLES W. KAY

Missouri, the Columbia and the Colorado. That a hydrographic apex is an obscure peak is not unique; Glacier Park's Triple Divide Peak (Gulf of Mexico, Hudson Bay and Pacific) and the Canadian Rockies' Snow Dome (Atlantic, Arctic, Pacific) hardly dominate their surroundings. Of more interest is the untangling of drainages you must do to convince yourself that Three Waters Mountain's waters do indeed reach the three great rivers.

It is important, in trying for an overview of the Wind Rivers—indeed of all Wyoming mountains—from the perspective of a satellite orbit 500 miles up, not to picture a pattern of stream systems determined by the layout of mountain chains. A closer look shows streams flowing in unexpected directions, making apparently capricious bends. The illogic of many streams in terms of present topography makes you curious about the geologic history of the region (while giving geologists clues about this same history).

Picture, then, the country west of Three Waters Mountain as an amorphous topography of low hills, crooked streams and marshes. The Wind Rivers more or less converge with the Absarokas to the north and the Gros Ventre Range to the west, and geology is required in order to delineate the boundaries of the three ranges. The 25 miles of Divide crest from Togwotee Pass to Three Waters Mountain is of little scenic interest, though Union Pass, midway along this section, is of some historic interest and much current environmental interest.

Northwest of Three Waters' summit are the headwaters of a minor stream named Fish Creek. After wandering across the haphazard topography south of Union Pass, Fish Creek joins the Gros Ventre River, which cuts through the mountains of the same name and joins the Snake River near the town of Jackson. The Snake is the Columbia's largest tributary; thus a little-known corner of the Wind Rivers lies in Columbia drainage.

The Roaring Fork, which drains the south slopes of Three Waters Mountain, joins a Green River that is emerging from the area of high peaks and glaciers flowing northwest. Just downstream, though, the Green bends sharply south and flows off across the plains to a rendezvous with the Colorado in Utah's canyonlands.

The northeast slope of Three Waters Mountain drains to the Wind River. The Wind River flows southeast until it makes a startling bend to the north, cuts through the Owl Creek Mountains, and emerges renamed the Bighorn River. The Bighorn flows to Montana and the Yellowstone River, which is in turn a Missouri River tributary.

The south end of the Wind Rivers offers another drainage anomaly. The range ends at South Pass, which is not a dramatic alpine gap but a broad, dry plain, beyond which are scattered low hills of the Red Desert. The Sweetwater River begins on the range's west slope but flows east. From the satellite perspective again, the Sweetwater appears to traverse South Pass, but this cannot be, for South Pass separates Atlantic waters from Pacific waters. The hydrographic location of the pass, the true height of land, is somewhat south and west of where the 100-mile-long

Above: *A rainbow precedes the clearing of a storm over the North Popo Agie, a few miles downstream from Lonesome Lake.* GEORGE WUERTHNER

Left: *Nine-mile-long Frémont Lake is the largest of several lakes formed by glacial gouging along the western base of the mountains. Beyond Frémont Lake, the plains of the Green River Valley extend to the Uinta and Wyoming ranges.* DENNIS J. CWIDAK

arrow that is the Wind Rivers' crest implies that it is. Nevertheless, while by definition the Sweetwater cannot cross the Continental Divide, its rounding the Wind River crest enabled the Oregon Trail to cross the Divide. For when covered wagons began crossing the continent, in the 1840s, the emigrants needed a gentle traverse from the Atlantic slope tó the Pacific slope, and they needed water every night.

Beyond South Pass, the Continental Divide splits in two—alternate versions going their own ways until they reunite near Rawlins and continue as one into Colorado. The geographic reality behind this quirk is the Great Divide Basin, a desert occupying a 50-by-75-mile area, which drains to neither ocean but rather retains what little water falls within.

The big rivers

Naming a large piece of rock for flowing water, which in turn is named for moving air, has proven both poetic and confusing. The river was named by the Crow Indians, although whether because the river sounds like wind or because it flows in a windy valley is uncertain. The river's name was casually applied to the mountains by the first white trappers in the area, in the early 1800s: the mountains beyond the Wind River. It is thus an accident that the name has given the mountains a reputation for windiness—a reputation they nevertheless deserve.

Neither the Indians nor the whites considered the stream that flows down the Wind River Valley and the stream that flows through the Bighorn Basin to be the same river, and today the one river retains its two names: Wind and Bighorn. The Crows, however, considered the Bighorn to begin at the bend, near modern Riverton, where the Wind River is joined by a river whose branches drain the east side of the southern Wind River Mountains. The Crows called this southern stream the Popo Agie, meaning "headwaters" (and pronounced "po-PO-zhia").

The name of the Green River has changed more frequently through time than along its course. Lewis referred to it as "River Colorado" and Clark as "Rio del Norte." The Astorians, in 1812, called it "Spanish River," for the territory was then Mexican, but the Mexicans called it "Rio Verde"—though whether because of shoreline vegetation or the color of the water is unknown. The Crows told early white

trappers that it was the "Seedskedie Agie"—the Prairie Hen River. By the 1830s, though, the Spanish name had been adopted and anglicized, and we know it as the Green.

The Sweetwater was not so named, as might be expected, because it was potable in a country notorious for bitter, alkaline water. The name was bestowed by one of the early trapping expeditions to reach the mountains via the North Platte and Sweetwater, when a mule fell into the river—the mule that happened to be carrying the company's supply of sugar.

However, most tributary streams that flow from the mountains to join the Wind River and Green River have neither such rich histories nor colorful names. Frémont reported camping on "the first New Fork" and had to explain that several tributaries of the Green were called New Forks. Today, only one New Fork remains, the northernmost one, a fine river that flows near Pinedale, while Frémont's first New Fork is now the East Fork River, and the streams between the two are distinguished with such names as Boulder Creek and Pine Creek.

Nomenclature is further impoverished farther into the mountains, where such streams as Boulder Creek and Bull Lake Creek, a major east-side stream, branch into a North Fork, a Middle Fork and a South Fork. It is possible to go west from the South Fork of the Little Wind River, over Washakie Pass, to the East Fork River and to climb north to a pass at the head of the East Fork and descend to the South Fork of Boulder Creek.

One of the Wind Rivers' noteworthy features occurs at valley level on both sides of the range, where many of the larger streams emerge from the mountains as long, thin, deep lakes. The largest of these is fed by Pine Creek, nine-mile-long Frémont Lake, which lies at 7,418' at the base of the western slope; Frémont Lake has been reported as the seventh deepest lake in the United States. Bull Lake on the east side is nearly as long, and New Fork Lakes, Willow Lake and Boulder Lake on the west side are all more than three miles long. The Green River emerges from the mountains through a pair of lakes, the Green River Lakes, which are an important entry point to the high country.

Above: Pinedale is a ranching community at the western base of the mountains offering unsurpassed sunset views of the Wind Rivers. Presumably in this vicinity, 19th-century trappers concluded that Frémont Peak (right) was the highest point in the Rockies. Gannett Peak, although higher, is hidden behind the peaks left of center. TOM TILL
Left: The headwaters of the range's rivers cascade from high in steep-walled cirques. Baptiste Creek, a source of the South Fork of the Little Wind River, begins below peaks such as Tower Peak, nearly hidden by Mt. Hooker's massive face, and an unnamed Divide summit farther up the valley. GEORGE WUERTHNER
Facing page: Clouds over the Green River Lakes obscure Squaretop, but the tilted strata of White Rock can be seen. LARRY ULRICH

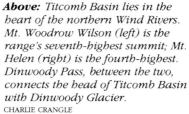

Above: Titcomb Basin lies in the heart of the northern Wind Rivers. Mt. Woodrow Wilson (left) is the range's seventh-highest summit; Mt. Helen (right) is the fourth-highest. Dinwoody Pass, between the two, connects the head of Titcomb Basin with Dinwoody Glacier.
CHARLIE CRANGLE

Right: *Like the Green River Valley west of the mountains, the Wind River Valley to the east is high desert. Red Canyon, near the town of Lander, is typical of the scenery in the lower Wind River Valley.*
BRUCE SELYEM

Facing page: *An aspen stand provides autumn color in the upper Green River Valley. The range's forest belt, mainly conifers, begins at a higher elevation.* TOM TILL

Wind Rivers geography

From Togwotee Pass to South Pass, in a straight line, is 110 miles. The width of the Wind Rivers is more arbitrary. From the meeting of sagebrush and forest on the west side to the meeting of sagebrush and forest on the east side is about 25 miles; this figure gives an idea of the extent of mountain country that is distinct from the plains.

The mountains are surrounded by highways on three sides. U.S. 191 parallels the range on the west side, in the Green River Valley, passing through the main west-side town—the ranching community of Pinedale—en route from Rock Springs to Jackson. On the east side, U.S. 287, which passes through the largest town in the region, Lander, joins U.S. 26 to ascend the Wind River past the other east-side town, Dubois, to Togwotee Pass and continue to Jackson Hole. U.S. 191 and U.S. 287 are connected by Wyoming 28, which crosses South Pass.

A road that is dirt for many miles follows the Green River past the tiny ranching community of Cora, near Pinedale,

to Green River Lakes, and a logging road connects this road, via Union Pass, with Dubois. But within the quadrilateral defined by the Green River Lakes-Union Pass roads and the three highways are no roads (except for a shortcut from South Pass to Lander) that do not end at the base of the mountains. These dead-end roads, however, lead to the approximately 15 trailheads, at elevations ranging from 7,139' to 9,520', that are the means of access to the high country.

Most of the Wind River high country is National Forest land that is designated wilderness. The Wind Rivers west of the Divide are the Bridger Wilderness of Bridger-Teton National Forest. The northern third of the Wind Rivers east of the Divide is the Fitzpatrick Wilderness of Shoshone National Forest, while the southern third is the Popo Agie Wilderness of Shoshone National Forest. The central third is a part of the Wind River Indian Reservation, which includes much of the Wind River Valley and is shared by Shoshones and Arapahos.

Weather patterns

A 100-mile chain of 13,000' peaks forms a barrier between weather regimes; annual precipitation statistics imply greater similarity between the east and west sides than in fact exists. Pinedale, at 7,180' on the west side, receives a yearly average of 9.11" (computed as rain). Dubois, across the range at 6,917', averages 9.35", and Lander, downstream on the east side at 5,563', averages 13.6". However, Lander and Dubois, in the Wind River Valley, receive more of their precipitation as spring and summer rain; Pinedale's precipitation is more evenly spread over the year, although with winter slightly wetter than summer.

The average temperature at Pinedale is 35°F. (Big Piney, on the Green River south of Pinedale, claims without opposition the distinction of being the "Icebox of Wyoming.") Dubois's mean temperature is 40°, while Lander's is 44°. Chinooks often warm the Wind River Valley in winter. When the Shoshones under Washakie, in 1868, requested a reservation, they asked for the Wind River Valley, which not only seemed to be out of the way of white migration but also, by Plains standards, was blessed with plentiful wood and water and an ideal climate.

Direct climatic data is not available for higher elevations. However, a geologist studying recent glaciation estimated temperatures in Titcomb Basin, using a formula developed empirically in other mountains. According to this formula, the mean yearly temperature at 10,500' in Titcomb Basin should be 26°F, with a January mean of 5° and a July mean of 49°.

Another scientist guesses that above 10,000' the Wind Rivers receive from 40" to 50" of precipitation per year.

Most summer moisture falls as rain, hail, or sleet during thunderstorms, which approach from the southwest. While no data is available on trends along the range from north to south, climbers have ample opportunity to observe that the high peaks around Dinwoody Glacier and Titcomb Basin attract a disproportionate share of electrical storms. The very southern end appears to be distinctly drier than the rest of the range, but also windier. South Pass no doubt acts as a funnel for the prevailing west winds.

ALONG THE DIVIDE

Above: *Petroglyphs, Wind River Valley.* BILL LANCASTER

Right: *The Divide attains two of its high points in Frémont Peak (left) and Jackson Peak (center), to the east of the ragged country that surrounds Seneca Lake.* PAT O'HARA

Driving north on the dirt road that follows the upper Green River, a traveler notes the stratified ridges of the Gros Ventre Range off to the left, the west. To the right, nearby foothills flecked with aspen groves block views of more distant scenery. The low rolling hills ahead, north, seem to be a gap between two mountain ranges. Then the road rounds the Green's Big Bend, turning southeast. The traveler, now passing between the aspen-covered foothills and such higher Divide peaks as Three Waters Mountain and seeing into the Green's canyon far ahead, for the first time has a sense of heading into the Wind Rivers. Actually, though, the gentle terrain north of the Big Bend is the northern end of the Wind Rivers.

While to geographers, geologists and a few loggers, hunters and fishers, the Wind Rivers begin at Togwotee Pass, this northern section is virtually unknown to climbers, hikers and photographers. To most recreational visitors, the range begins 30 miles south of Togwotee Pass at Green River Lakes, and when we speak of the northern Wind Rivers, we mean country south or east of Green River Lakes and Three Waters Mountain.

The road ends at a campground and trailhead parking lot just north of Lower Green River Lake. The view from here is the best known in the Wind Rivers. Seemingly looming above the green waters of the lake—though actually eight miles upstream—is a formation shaped less like a mountain than like a tree stump. Squaretop Mountain, with a summit 3,734' above the lake, 11,695' above sea level and half a mile across, is used as a symbol of the entire range more often than higher, more graceful peaks. This choice of symbol, based largely on accessibility of the viewpoint by car, is unfortunate, but not because of Squaretop's uninspiring shape. The Wind Rivers are not a range of Matterhorns and Grand Tetons; the peaks in general give the impression of a sculptor quitting before the job was done. Rather, Squaretop is an atypical Wind River peak because it *is* so visible from a car window and because of its claustrophobic position, flanked on one side by the narrow gorge of the Green River, on the other side

by the tight little cirque of Marten Lake. Through most of the range a visitor's spirits are less likely to be raised by soaring spires than by the openness of the country, the vast skies.

The walls of Squaretop are steep, but by continuing up the Green River past the walls, it is possible to reach the summit plateau by unroped scrambling. The top of Squaretop is a good place from which to see the northern part of the range.

One topographic feature dominates this end of the range, simply by its strangeness—the flatness of the land at about 12,000'. There are no peaks in this area, only flats of varying breadths. Other formations are named Tabletop and Flat Top, and there is a Square Top east of the Divide. Squaretop (not to mention Square Top) is seen to be a minor example of a planar surface. Four or five square miles of a plateau straddling the Divide northeast of Squaretop, part of which is known as Ram Flat and part as Shale Mountain, lie above 12,000', with no point exceeding 12,262'. In the northern Wind Rivers, one rounded, gentle-sloped summit rises above the plateaus: 13,349' Downs' Mountain, the highest point within five miles.

The most celebrated Wind River scene features a formation that is neither high, snow-mantled, nor sharp-summited. Nevertheless, Squaretop, a remnant of an erosion surface that before the ice ages covered much of Wyoming, dominates the Green River Lakes as no other Wind River peak dominates its surroundings. JEFF GNASS

Wyoming's highest point, snow-capped Gannett Peak, rises amid extensive glacier systems on both sides of the Divide. This view shows Gannett Glacier descending the peak's northeast side. Among the several surrounding peaks that are nearly as high as Gannett is the range's third-highest peak, Mt. Warren (left of center). Farther left are gently sloping remnants of the once-continuous erosion surface.
M. VIDAK

The highest point in Wyoming is 13,804' Gannett Peak, 34' higher than the better-known Grand Teton and 59' higher than nearby Frémont Peak, which through the 19th century was believed to be the highest Wind River summit. Gannett's relative obscurity is attributable to the number of peaks nearly as high that surround it. From the Wind River Valley to the east, Gannett is hidden behind the long slope of Horse Ridge, which rises to over 13,000'. From the west, from the Green River Valley, Gannett's snow-covered top may be seen from many places, but only through a notch between apparently higher foreground peaks. From the south it is seen as one of a sea of high summits. Only from the west, from Squaretop, does Gannett's whalelike profile stand prominent on the crest.

Yet Gannett is an elegant peak, largely because of its mantle of snow. Its summit ridge is crested with snow, and on the east side, Gannett, Gooseneck and Dinwoody glaciers reach high on its flanks, while below its west face lie Mammoth and Minor glaciers. Because of its glaciers, as well as its height, Gannett is a popular objective for mountaineers, despite an approach hike of more than 20 miles either from the east or the west. (No ascent of Gannett was reported until 1922, although the Grand Teton and Frémont Peak were climbed in the 1800s, with publicity and controversy.)

The area dominated by Gannett and Frémont peaks consists of high peaks surrounding four principal basins— one each facing north, south, west and east. The west-facing and south-facing basins, predictably, contain smaller glaciers than the north-facing basin, occupied by Dinwoody, Gooseneck and Gannett glaciers, all drained by Dinwoody Creek and the east-facing basin.

The western valley, named for Peak Lake at its lower end, is the least dramatic scenically and the least visited, but does have one geographic distinction. During the last century the Green River was considered the main stream of the Colorado, while what is now the Colorado, above its confluence with the Green was the Grand River. In Three Forks Park, below Squaretop, three streams cascade down from the high country to form the Green. Two are Trail Creek and Wells Creek, which drains Mammoth and Minor glaciers. The middle stream, which descends from Peak Lake, is considered the Green. In the 1930s the U.S. Board on Geographic Names decreed the creek that carries the

Nevertheless, this is rugged country, seldom visited. The plateaus are separated by steep, narrow canyons. In a range not noted for waterfalls (on the topographic maps, only five are named), streams cascade stepwise down thousand-foot drops, and their canyons are difficult to ascend. Topographic maps contain legends that explain how roads and trails are represented. On the Downs' Mountain quadrangle it simply says, "No roads or trails in this area."

High peaks

The view southeast from Squaretop is markedly different. Twenty-six Wyoming peaks stand above 13,000' (and rise at least 500' from any saddle connecting them to a higher peak). One is in the Tetons, one in the Absarokas, one in the Bighorns and 23 in the Wind Rivers. Twenty-one of these are within nine miles of one another on or near the Divide southeast of Squaretop. Relax the 500'-rise criterion and the topographic maps contain an additional 11 named 13,000' summits.

meltwaters of Stroud Glacier, a pocket of permanent snow above Peak Lake, to be the headwaters of the Green. The identity of a river's true source is a matter of arbitrary nomenclature, yet in the past it was important, at least to explorers seeking the sources of such rivers as the Nile and the Mississippi.

If scenery could be quantified and graphed, the Wind Rivers would appear as a classic suspension bridge—the Golden Gate, the George Washington. The northern tower would stand at Dinwoody Pass, which connects Dinwoody Glacier, at the base of Gannett, with Titcomb Basin, tucked at the base of Frémont Peak, the range's most conspicuous mountain.

Titcomb Basin is a narrow, five-mile-long lake-filled valley, which descends from 12,800′ Dinwoody Pass, first steeply, then gradually, to 10,346′ Island Lake. The east side of Titcomb Basin is formed by one of the range's highest, steepest escarpments—the 2,000′ to 3,000′ west faces of 13,620′ Mt. Helen, 13,569′ Mt. Sacagawea and Frémont Peak. Titcomb Basin is one of the Wind Rivers' popular sites for climbing base camps.

A minor ridge runs south from Frémont Peak toward Island Lake, separating Titcomb Basin from a smaller lake-filled valley, Indian Basin, which also is ringed by 13,000′ peaks—Frémont again, 13,517′ Jackson Peak, 13,001′ Knife Point Mountain and a 13,052′ peak that, despite a political name change to Harrower, climbers persist in calling it Ellingwood, for a gallant 1920s mountaineer who first climbed it and pioneered many other early routes in the area.

Indian Basin derived its name from Indian Pass at its head, which despite its 12,120′ elevation, was a main route over the Divide before the coming of whites. Despite a century of rock slides and avalanches, Indian rock work is still barely visible. Indian Pass leads to the main east-flowing drainage of the high peaks area, that of Bull Lake Creek. This remote, trailless, rarely traveled drainage begins at a series of glaciers tucked under the east side of the Divide. The glaciers—Helen, Sacagawea, Upper Frémont, Lower Frémont, Bull Lake and Knife Point—lap so high on the east flanks of the Divide peaks that the great west faces of the peaks may be imagined to be false fronts created for a stage set.

The glaciers drained by Bull Lake Creek are separated from Dinwoody drainage by another row of high summits, including 13,722′ Mt. Warren, the range's third highest point and 13,600′ Turret Peak, the fifth highest.

Frémont Peak is a popular objective for hikers and climbers. Ascents typically begin from a camp at one of the unnamed lakes above Island Lake—where Frémont and his men began their 1842 ascent. JOE KELSEY

Early autumn snow leaves Mt. St. Michel and Mt. Bonneville white for a few days—or through winter if other storms follow closely. M. VIDAK

Gentler Terrain

The high peaks rise above the 12,000′ plateaus. To the south of the jagged spine of Knife Point Mountain, however, the Divide again becomes strangely flat and broad, though neither as horizontal nor as extensive as the surfaces around Downs' Mountain. The country west of the Divide becomes high rolling upland, less dramatic, less urgent-seeming than the basins just to the north. The appeal of this midsection of the Wind Rivers is not the peaks, which are rarely climbed, but the numerous west-side lakes—some, like Cook Lakes, noted for fish, others too high for fish.

The Wind River high country is more frequently approached from the west than from the east, especially in the middle part, where the Wind River Indians do not maintain a trail system, as the Forest Service does elsewhere, and can discourage would-be visitors with a cumbersome permit system. No maintained trails reach the area south of the Bull Lake glaciers from the Wind River

Valley, and the high but nearly level Divide ridge does not inspire a hiker at Cook Lakes to see what is on the other side. Yet the Divide conceals one of the most rugged parts of the Wind Rivers and the heart of what mystery the range retains. Even the view from, say, Frémont Peak reveals only more flat-topped formations, but while these peaks are broad, the valleys between are narrow. Climbers did not visit the area until the 1960s; until 1968, the three Alpine Lakes, which along with the Brown Cliffs were the only geographic features named on the topographic map, were connected incorrectly on the map.

For 17 miles south of Knife Point Mountain the array of gentle, obscure peaks along, and west of, the Divide continues—Mt. Baldy, Angel Peak, Round Top Mountain, Mt. Victor, Medina Mountain, Europe Peak, Hall's Mountain (at 12,475′ the highest of these). At Middle Fork Lake, though, the terrain again comes to life—or at least brings a climber to life.

Mile-and-a-half-long Middle Fork Lake, at 10,252′, makes a typical Wind River climbing base—a scattering of trees but mostly open meadows, with views of both broad, low-angle peaks and sharp, steep peaks. The view south from Middle Fork Lake is one of the range's classics: between the tent-shaped massif known both as Mont Saint Michel and Nylon Peak (named when nylon climbing rope first became available) on the left and the near-vertical east faces of Dragon Head and Pronghorn peaks on the right stands one of the Wind Rivers' most easily recognized peaks, Mt. Bonneville. Bonneville is a jagged mile-long crest running southwest from the main Divide to separate the head of the South Fork of Boulder Creek from the head of the East Fork River. It owes its familiarity to climbers and hikers to its conspicuous position off the Divide but at the head of two drainages, and also to its symmetrical shape when seen from either north or south. The 12,585′ summit, a pyramidal beak, is flanked by two ridges, each with a subsummit that gives its ridge the angled silhouette of a bird of prey—perhaps a prairie falcon such as nests on nearby cliffs or an osprey seen nesting on a telephone pole along the lower reaches of the East Fork or Boulder Creek.

Across the Divide east of Middle Fork Lake the skyline is dominated by two rambling plateau segments, 12,631′ Wolverine Peak and 12,767′ Roberts' Mountain, which

despite their extensive summit areas are largely flanked by vertical walls. The lower terrain is dominated by lakes; within the four-by-six-mile valley bounded by Wolverine and Roberts', the North Fork of the Little Wind River's drainage, are nine lakes at least a half-mile long and many smaller ones.

The walls of Wolverine and Roberts', and of Dragon Head, Pronghorn and Bonneville, portend rugged country to the south. Bonneville, a scenic centerpiece from both north and south, may be considered to mark the transition from the central Wind Rivers to the southern Wind Rivers. If one tower of the scenery-quantifying suspension bridge would stand at Dinwoody Pass, the other tower would stand 30 miles to the south, eight miles south of Mt. Bonneville. The suspension bridge analogy must not be taken to imply a topographic symmetry from north to south; while the northern peaks are noteworthy for being high and snow-covered, the southern peaks are noteworthy for being steep and rocky.

Top left: Peak Lake (partly obscured by the foreground summit rocks of Stroud Peak) and Stonehammer Lake (middle distance). Squaretop can be seen left of the Green's canyon, sedimentary White Rock to the right. CHARLIE CRANGLE ***Above:*** *South of Middle Fork Lake (foreground). Mt. St. Michel (left) stands just off the Divide, while the jagged ridges of Mt. Bonneville extend west from the crest. Pronghorn and Dragon Head (right) are typical of the range's westernmost peaks in that they present steep walls to the east, low-angle rubble slopes to the west.* M. VIDAK
Left: *The East Fork River heads in a flat valley enclosed by the Divide (foreground) and some of the biggest walls in the American Rockies, such as those of Ambush Peak (left) and Raid Peak (right).* GEORGE WUERTHNER

19

Above: *Cirque of the Towers, in the center of which lies Lonesome Lake. In this view two unnamed peaks are flanked by the shaded wall of Pingora (left) and a ridge of Camel's Hump (right).*
JEFF GNASS
Facing page: *The two most popular climbing objects in Cirque of the Towers are Pingora (right) and Wolf's Head (center).* PAT O'HARA

The Cirque of the Towers

During the 1920s and 1930s, climbers concentrated on the peaks around Dinwoody Glacier and Titcomb Basin. These pioneers were transplanting mountaineering from the Alps, and the northern Wind Rivers offered the most alpine terrain.

Three locals reached the south summit of Bonneville in 1927, declaring the main summit impossible, but another attempt was not reported until a successful ascent in 1946. Only sheepherders, fishermen, solitary wanderers without vertical ambition, and a few curious mountaineers more intent on exploring than climbing probed the southern Wind Rivers before 1940. When the alpinists tried to describe to their brotherhood what they had seen, they were hindered by a paucity of nomenclature. There were no topographic maps until 1938, and the 1938 maps named only a few peaks and lakes. Such locally used names as "Dad's Toothpicks," which west-side travelers applied to the curiously serrated Divide ridge at the head of Washakie Creek, were of little help. Explorers could describe passing only so many unnamed lakes, crossing so many nameless passes and beholding so many anonymous peaks without losing both themselves and their readers.

In 1940, Orrin Bonney and two companions found their way up the North Popo Agie to its little-known head at a 10,166' lake, which the map named Lonesome Lake. Inspired by rumors of a semicircle of rock towers, they came equipped with what must have been the first climbing ropes and hardware brought to this remote locale. From meadows north of the lake rose the highest peak between them and Knife Point Mountain, 12,842' Lizard Head—which, however, on this side is not a tower but a broad, messy complex of gullies, slabs and scree. Anticipating a first ascent, the three climbed Lizard Head, only to find two scraps of paper bearing illegible names.

Standing off the semicircular Divide, rising directly from Lonesome Lake for 1,718', was a tower with no easy side. One evening the climbers declared it impossible—and ascended it the next day. Bonney returned in 1941 and climbed the tower at the southern end of the chain. From its summit, he made an interesting discovery—that Lonesome Lake could be reached from the Big Sandy River, on the west side of the range, by way of a pass below his feet. He described what he had seen and climbed in mountaineering journals, naming the tower above Lonesome Lake Pingora, Shoshone for "high, rocky, inaccessible peak," the 1941 peak Warbonnet, the Divide crossing below it Jackass Pass and the bowl the Cirque of the Towers.

More climbers began visiting the Cirque of the Towers, some via Jackass Pass, some by camping at Shadow Lake,

under the west faces of the Divide towers. Bonney had given the name Camel's Hump to the summit next to Lizard Head, and this anatomical terminology spread, as Shadow Lake climbers named two of the finest towers Wolf's Head and Shark's Nose (while their neighbors became more prosaic Overhanging Tower, Block Tower and Watch Tower).

Pingora might seem to have little to attract humanity's attention. It is lower (11,884') than surrounding peaks and invisible from civilization and even from trailhead parking lots. Compared to the celebrated spires of the world—to Shark's Nose, Wolf's Head and Overhanging Tower in fact—it is distinctly flat-topped. Yet today Pingora, despite or because of its difficulty, is the most-climbed peak in the Wind Rivers. In Steve Roper's and Allen Steck's *Fifty Classic Climbs of North America,* Pingora's Northeast Face and Wolf's Head's East Ridge are two of the 50.

Climbers are forever scanning horizons for more to climb, and from Cirque summits can be seen to the north, toward Mt. Bonneville, many high, steep walls. From the west end of Bonneville a ridge runs south, separated from the Divide by the deep valley of the upper East Fork. The east faces of the three summits on this ridge—Raid, Ambush and Geikie—are among the most impressive in the range, although the west slopes are low-angle and grassy, no more than strenuous hikes.

Much of the Divide between Bonneville and the Cirque of the Towers consists of massive, rubbly hulks, but there is one dramatic exception, even if this exception is not apparent from west of the Divide. Mt. Hooker, seen from the west as another rounded profile, with its several-acre, 12,504' summit a plateau segment that includes streams, flower patches and a pond, nevertheless has a complex architecture of north and east faces that, in climbers' imprecise parlance, forms the "biggest wall" in the American Rockies—1,600' and dead vertical. After its discovery by admiring climbers in the Cirque of the Towers and a few unsuccessful attempts to climb it, the North Face of Hooker required three and a half days for its first ascent, in 1964.

Hooker is out of the way and hard to reach, but climbers en route to the Cirque of the Towers via the Big Sandy River, Big Sandy Lake and Jackass Pass have a good

opportunity to study formations south of Big Sandy Lake. Three parallel valleys drain north to Big Sandy Lake. The easternmost, nearest the Divide, is narrow, boulder-strewn and filled from wall to wall by Black Joe Lake. The middle of the three flows from Deep Lake past Clear Lake over polished bedrock slabs, short falls alternating with pools that reflect the mile-long west face of the 11,978′ formation named Haystack Mountain, although "mountain" does not properly categorize its summitless shape. Above Deep Lake is the unmistakable form of 12,600′ East Temple Peak, vertical east and north walls converging at a prow that sweeps up to a gentle-sloped field of angular blocks. The western of the three valleys is drained by Rapid Creek, which heads in a pocket glacier beneath the classic concave alpine north face of Temple Peak, at 12,972′ the second highest of the southern Wind Rivers. To many climbers, these valleys, Deep Lake's in particular, are an appendage of the Cirque of the Towers.

South of the Cirque of the Towers, the Divide rises from Jackass Pass to steep-walled Mitchell Peak, named for legendary Finis Mitchell, who has been exploring the Wind Rivers since 1909, planted fish in hundreds of the lakes, and climbed his peak 11 times. To the south of Mitchell

Peak, the Divide reverts to another extensive plateau—although enough cirques are cut into its flanks that geologists call it the "Biscuit Board." This plateau culminates, five miles south of Jackass Pass, in the highest summit in the southern Wind Rivers, 13,192′ Wind River Peak. That a peak distinguished by little but its height, similar to Downs' Mountain, should be designated *the* Wind River Peak may seem odd, especially to someone who only has seen its rounded dome in summer, free of snow. But to emigrants of the 1840s (when summers were cooler), struggling to get their covered wagons up the Sweetwater River, the ruggedest part of the Oregon Trail, it must have seemed like much more than the Wind River Peak.

South of Wind River Peak, the mountains gradually dwindle. Three summits—Mt. Nystrom, West Atlantic Peak and Atlantic Peak—are worthy of names, but the southernmost summits are wooded. One, 10,261′ Pabst Peak, was named because the Titcomb Brothers returned to then-functioning South Pass City in 1901 and reported drinking a bottle of beer on top. The bottle was found in 1972, perhaps indicating either obliviousness to litter or respect for artifacts on the part of climbers, but more likely showing how little-traveled this tip of the range is.

Above: *Clear Lake, south of the Cirque of the Towers, makes a convenient base camp for climbers attracted by the mile-wide cliffs of Haystack Mountain.* DENNIS J. CWIDAK
Left: *A backpacker approaches the Cirque of the Towers from the north, by Texas Pass. Ahead lie Warbonnet (left) and the Warriors (right).* DENNIS J. CWIDAK
Facing page: *While the Cirque of the Towers is the most popular climbers' playground, the range's greatest challenge is Mt. Hooker's 1600′ North Face, which required four days for its first ascent.* GEORGE WUERTHNER

GEOLOGY

Above: *The swirls, colors and chunks in Wind River gneiss suggest the story of the rock's creation—intruding magma, partially melted older rock, pressures from different directions.*
Right: *A late-afternoon storm passes Ellingwood Peak, near Island Lake.*
JOE KELSEY PHOTOS

S cenery has a subjective effect on the beholder, and we trick ourselves by attributing to a scene the mood it inspires in ourselves. We think of the soaring alpine peaks of Titcomb Basin, of sharp, symmetrical Mt. Bonneville, of the jagged Cirque of the Towers, as fresh, vigorous, proud. The midsection of the range, from Cook Lakes to Middle Fork Lake, despite a lack of postcard grandeur, also affects our emotions, although differently than the higher, sharper terrain. The broad, open valleys, rambling topography, many lakes and vast skies tend to evoke serenity, contemplation. The scattered summits of Medina Mountain, Mt. Victor, Angel Peak, Mt. Baldy—broad, grass-and-rubble-sloped, curved rather than angular ridges—can themselves seem quietly contemplative, perhaps during a storm stoically brooding. Whatever our mood may be, they seem to stand with imperturbable dignity—above all, with stability.

The big picture

The attribution of emotions to inanimate rock has no place in geology, of course. It is thus coincidence that Medina Mountain rock happens to be composed of material that has been part of the earth's crust for 3.4 billion years—a bit younger than the oldest crust yet found on earth, Greenland rock dated at 3.7 to 3.8 billion years old. (Isotopic dating indicates the time at which material transferred from the mantle to the crust; it is crust of which continents are made.) However, this 3.4 billion-year-old rock is uncut by dikes that cut adjacent rock. The implication to geologists is that the adjacent rock—a band extending west from Hall's Lake, near the Divide, to the edge of the Wind Rivers—existed when the dikes formed, while the 3.4 billion-year-old rock did not. There is recent evidence that crystals in the older rock formed in the crust 3.8 billion years ago.

If there is a contest for antiquity, the Wind Rivers' close competition comes from the Beartooths, but it is not a distinction that interests geologists. That Medina Mountain rock turns out to be older than, say, Frémont Peak rock is the result of many recent geological quirks. What is more interesting is reconstructing the North American continent, perhaps the planet in its early days. For these larger-scale purposes, the Wind Rivers and Beartooths are both part of

the ancient Wyoming Province, a block that includes nearly all of Wyoming plus the Black Hills to the east, the Beartooths to the north, the Wasatch in Utah to the southwest, and the mountains of Idaho as far as the Raft River Range.

Climbers are attracted to the Wind Rivers by the magic word *granite*. Granite (including igneous rocks similar to granite although mineralogically distinguishable) is the main component of the range's core, but the rock of the Wyoming Province existed for nearly a billion years before the molten magma that became this granite intruded into and around it.

To trace this rock to its origins is pushing geology to its limits, and geologists are careful to qualify conjectures with such phrases as "it seems likely." It seems likely that most of the oldest rock was once sedimentary rock that partially melted deep below the surface—probably five to 10 miles down, at temperatures greater than 1400°F (765°C). Some,

Ice-age glaciers left evidence of their existence in both the rock they eroded and the rock they deposited. Near Washakie Lake, glaciers steepened headwalls, polished bedrock, and dropped angular blocks carried from upvalley.
GEORGE WUERTHNER

Above: *Long after an ice age, lichen forms on glacially deposited boulders, soil develops, and flowering plants return, as columbine, bluebells and the pungent polemonium species known as skunkflower have in this meadow.* JEFF GNASS

Facing page: *Glaciers still exist high in Titcomb Basin, but the U-shaped cross-section indicates that the basin was formerly occupied by far greater bodies of moving ice.* PAT O'HARA

though, may have been pre-existing granite; some may have been volcanic. Under deep pressures, the melted part recrystallized as a granitic phase; the part that did not melt was nevertheless hot enough to flow plastically and, subjected to complex pressures, metamorphosed into streaks, swirls and wisps of *gneiss*. Gneiss includes the same minerals as granite, but with layers containing different proportions of these minerals—light-colored bands rich in quartz and feldspar, dark-colored bands rich in biotite and hornblende. These layers reflect not only the texture of the original rock but conditions during its metamorphism—that it did not form from a homogeneous melt, that it was squeezed by unequal compressive forces. The resulting mixture of gneiss and granite, called *migmatite,* is the oldest rock in the Wind Rivers.

A second episode of deep burial, with temperatures and pressures similar to the first, included sedimentary rock with the older migmatite. The sediments had been derived since the first metamorphism by surface weathering, transport and deposition of the crustal material that is now 3.4 billion years old. The migmatite was further metamorphosed; the sedimentary rock became gneiss such as that found on Medina Mountain.

Toward the end of the second metamorphism, 2.7 billion years ago, the existing gneisses and migmatites were engulfed by molten material—*magma*—that, when it cooled, crystallized into granite. Not many years ago, geologists would have been content to know that the rock came from magma, rather than lava or sediments. However, their science now has evolved to the point that they wonder where the magma came from. The best guess is the magma that intruded existing rock 2.7 billion years ago was derived partly from material in the mantle, partly from recycled crust—just as magma still is produced when two continents collide, one is forced down, and its leading edge melts below the overriding continent.

The distinction between igneous and metamorphic rock is clearer in a textbook than in the area north of Mt. Victor and Medina Mountain. The hot intruding magma did not simply solidify as granite next to the existing gneiss. It melted the older rock and further metamorphosed and deformed it by heat, by pressure and by chemically reacting with it. Liquid flowed into cracks; gneissic chunks dropped into the granitic soup.

A hiker can study a single chunk in Titcomb Basin, near Middle Fork Lake, near Baptiste Lake, and, while being reminded of an ice cream concoction, envision the rock's formation. One can imagine temperatures high enough to soften the rock so that it could be folded over, without breaking, like chocolate on a warm day, and imagine the sequence of pressures that resulted in such complex deformation of the gneissic layers. One can see in the fuzzy contact zones between gneiss and granite the chemical effect of one on the other. Here are phrases geologists have used to describe exposures of migmatite: "alternating dark and light stripes, swirling around in complex patterns," "layers...stretched and separated by flowage into lenses, wisps and streaks," "soupy," "swirly and chaotic." Bedrock north of Medina Mountain has appeared on geologic maps as gneiss, as granite and as migmatite.

Again, 2.6 billion years ago, magma intruded the Wind River block. This magma crystallized as dark granitic rock, technically granodiorite. While the main exposure of this granodiorite is from Wind River Peak south, smaller outcrops have been found as far north as Grave Lake and near Medina Mountain.

A third and final invasion by magma occurred 2.5 billion years ago, forming the resistant, resilient granite for which the Cirque of the Towers is noted, as well as less-celebrated exposures north of Frémont Lake and east of Downs' Mountain.

These magmatic emplacements were accompanied by further metamorphism of existing rock, but during the 2.5 billion years since, the crystalline core of the Wind Rivers hardly has changed. The gneisses, granites and migmatites we walk on have survived for more than half the duration of the earth.

In the interim

Little is known about the block that eventually became the Wind Rivers after the granitic intrusions and before 600 million years ago. Mountains may have risen and been worn down, but 600 million years ago western Wyoming was a gently rolling plain that drained west to a sea that covered parts of Idaho, Utah, Nevada and southern California. Then western Wyoming subsided, and the sea advanced eastward over the land.

Sand beaches were deposited at the edge of the sea. As the sea continued advancing east, mud and, later, carbonates were deposited over the sand. Subsequent compression compacted these sediments into sedimentary rock: sand as *sandstone*, mud as *shale*, carbonates as *limestone* and *dolomite*. These sandstones, shales, limestones and dolomites covered the gneisses, granites and migmatites.

Laramide revolution

The event that made it possible for geologists to study rock billions of years old occurred recently: within the past 65

Above: Elephant Head, seen here from Indian Basin, is formed of resistant rock, so that while glaciers could not obliterate it, they did steepen its sides. CHARLIE CRANGLE

Right: When glaciers carve cirques into opposite sides of a peak, the classic result is a narrow, serrated ridge. The long ridge of Haystack Mountain and the North Ridge of Steeple Peak, whose summit the climber is nearing, separate the valleys of Deep Lake and Black Joe Lake. M. VIDAK

million years. The event is known as the Laramide Revolution. The crystalline core of the Wind Rivers 65 million years ago lay beneath sediments that were just emerging from the sea. But horizontal compressive forces had been buckling the crust to the west, and this disturbance progressed eastward, wavelike. Where the crust bowed upward, mountains formed; where it bowed down, valleys. To the west of the Wind Rivers, pieces of crust were thrust miles out over other pieces.

The Laramide Revolution reached the future Wind River Mountains 65 million years ago. The rock was pushed up as an arch. As folding progressed, the arch developed asymmetrically, leaning west, and began to overturn. Fifty-five million years ago, it reached its breaking point.

Sometime between the intrusion of granite 2.5 billion years ago and the deposition of sediments 600 million years ago, the block had been broken by a series of *faults*—lines along which one side of the fractured block moved relative to the other. The most prominent faults paralleled the present northwest-southeast axis of the range. The shearing forces that caused faulting also altered minerals that recemented fractures, but these faults were planes of weakness, and when mountain-building forces were strong enough, the block refractured along these old lines.

During the Laramide Revolution, the Wind Rivers were pushed up along vertical fault lines and thrust out to the west along at least two lower-angle faults. One of these thrust faults passes east of New Fork Lakes; the evidence is plain at the mouth of New Fork Canyon, where gneiss and granite were thrust up over younger sandstone. Another thrust fault is followed by the Green River between Three Forks Park and Beaver Park. Over a million years, the Wind River block inched several miles southwest.

Asymmetrical arching, accentuated by overthrusting to the southwest, produced a range with an asymmetrical cross-section. On the southwest side, much of the sedimentary rock that covered the crystalline core was buried, while on the northeast side, the strata were left tilted in long, gentle slopes. Tilting and overthrusting are responsible for the mountains' being more impressive when seen from the west rather than from the east.

Overthrusting also has interested economic geologists. Traditionally they did not look for fossil fuels under granite, but the discovery of oil reserves under the overthrust mountains southwest of the Wind Rivers has sparked their curiosity about the precise geometry of the uplift. So far, however, the Wind Rivers have been spared any dramatic oil discovery.

Uplift & erosion

Relative to the Wind River and Green River valleys, the block rose on the order of 60,000'—one of the greatest vertical movements known on earth. The Laramide Revolution, however, did not create 60,000' mountains. Even while uplift continued, streams were lowering the mountains and filling the valleys; indeed, the steeper the rise, the more vigorous was the streams' erosive power.

Sedimentary rocks soon were removed from much of the block, exposing the underlying granite, gneiss and migmatite. Sandstone, shale, limestone and dolomite survive only on certain peaks around Green River Lakes— Big Sheep Mountain, White Rock—and on the long east-side ridges, such as Horse Ridge. Sedimentary rocks are an unimportant part of the Wind River story.

Erosion lowered the mountains and filled the valleys for a long enough time, without a disturbance of the crust producing further uplift, that the ancestral Wind Rivers were reduced to a gently rolling plain, protected from further lowering because the sediments accumulated in the valleys up to the same level. The Absaroka, Beartooth, Bighorn,

Medicine Bow and Granite mountains were similarly worn down; by 10 million years ago, 90 per cent of Wyoming, along with bits of Colorado and Nebraska, was one vast plain. Only a few rounded peaks protruded from the plain here and there. The crystalline cores of the ranges still existed, but they had been buried.

One effect of this burial was that the mountains did not determine the direction in which rivers—in stream beds thousands of feet higher than they are now—wandered over the plains. Stream courses were determined by surface topography, not by resistant granite below the surface. The Wind River, which had continued east as a

Much engineering design is based on the principle that three legs provide a stable base for a table. Glacially deposited debris can be distinguished from stream deposits by its angularity (streams round rocks) and by a lack of sorting according to size.
JOHN McCONNELL

tributary of the Sweetwater, instead crossed the buried Owl Creek Mountains into the Bighorn Basin. The Sweetwater cut back over the buried southern end of the Wind Rivers, moving the Continental Divide west and, in effect, creating the Oregon Trail. When the mountains again rose, streams continued eroding downward; the Wind River, for instance, cut its way into the core of the Owl Creeks.

During the past 10 million years, the Wind Rivers and the other ranges have been exhumed. The entire region was elevated farther above sea level than it had been. This gave new life to the previously sluggish streams, which carried away much of the debris that had accumulated on the mountains' flanks during burial.

When the Wind Rivers again stood out above the valleys, however, the core did not emerge as a row of jagged peaks. The block, having been flattened into part of the plain, rose above 12,000′ retaining its horizontal crest, which survives today as the vast plateaus of Ram Flat and Goat Flat and as such less-extensive remnants as Squaretop. In an inversion of usual mountain topography, the flattest areas of the Wind Rivers, the whitest parts of topographic maps, lie at the higher elevations. These plateaus once were called *peneplains,* but this word is now somewhat in disrepute, and the more acceptable current terms are the blander *erosion surface* and *subsummit surface.*

The erosion surface has been worn away at its edges but is otherwise singularly immune to erosion. Frost shatters the bedrock into blocks, but streams cannot transport the rock across such flat terrain—streams, moreover, that are too near their headwaters to have acquired upstream velocity. The frost-shattered, angular blocks accumulate in fields of *felsenmeer*—seas of rock. When scientists wanted to study the long-term effect of cosmic radiation on rock, they chose the erosion surface near the north end of the Wind Rivers, where rock has been exposed virtually since the Laramide Revolution.

The Wind Rivers were not uncovered by a continuous rise of the country but by episodes of uplift punctuated with pauses. The intermittent nature of this process has had a profound effect on mankind's relation to the Wind Rivers, especially on the west side.

In the view from the Green River Valley, the original erosion surface forms the range's horizon, but below the horizon can be seen a series of steps or terraces. These terraces are a result of the uplifts of the past 10 million years. When streams were rejuvenated as mountains re-emerged above the plains, they eroded most vigorously toward the bottom of gradients. With their lower reaches flattening first, they developed characteristic concave profiles, steeper near the head than downstream. Pauses during uplift gave the streams time to reduce the flanks of the mountains to what was then the level of the plains. Before the second of the recent uplifts, the unique terrace that extends along the west side from Doubletop Mountain to Big Sandy Opening had been created. These streams also began carving valleys back toward the Divide—the valleys of Dinwoody and Frémont creeks, of the North Popo Agie, the Big Sandy and the East Fork—valleys that would become the most-popular base-camp sites.

When uplift resumed, this country rose with the mountains, but the process of stream erosion was repeated below it and another terrace formed. The cycle appears to have been repeated five times, the lowest surface merging into the Green River Basin.

Incidentally, the uncovering of the Wind Rivers has influenced today's trail system. The ancient fault lines, reactivated during the Laramide Revolution, are zones of shattered rock, more easily eroded than the massive, unfractured rock. Streams tend to develop courses where the rock is most easily eroded, and the presence of a stream further hastens erosion, accentuating a zone of weakness. Thus an anomalous number of Wind River creeks flow not with the general slope of the land but at right angles to it, parallel to the crest. Travel parallel to the crest of the Wind Rivers is consequently easier than in most ranges.

Above: The summit plateaus of Mts. Hooker (right) and Chauvenet (left distance), which stand in strong contrast to steep, glacier-carved walls, are probably remnants of the vast erosion surface that existed before the ice ages. CHARLIE CRANGLE
Left: Peak Lake owes its blue tint to suspended particles of rock "flour," finely ground just upstream by Stroud Glacier. Stroud Glacier has been designated by the U.S. Board on Geographic Names as the source of the Green River. CHARLIE CRANGLE
Facing page: During one of the ice ages a glacier filled the valley of the Green River to the base of Square-top's walls (seen in foreground), 2,500' above the present river.
SPENCER SWANGER; TOM STACK & ASSOCIATES

Ice ages

As recently as 1 million years ago, the Wind Rivers displayed little of their present ruggedness. They were high but gentle-sloped hills, as the upper slopes of Downs' Mountain and Wind River Peak are today. Streams had created valleys approximately where streams flow today, but the valleys were narrower, with V-shaped cross sections. Frémont Lake, Bull Lake, the Green River Lakes and the other large foothill lakes did not exist, nor did Lonesome Lake, Peak Lake, Shadow Lake or the Titcomb Lakes. Then the climate changed.

Several times during the past 250,000 years, for periods of thousands of years, temperatures averaged a few degrees below normal. During each cooling episode, ice spread from the poles. Polar ice sheets did not reach as far south as Wyoming, but ice caps formed over the high ranges; the largest ice cap covered the extensive high country of the Wind Rivers. Glaciers flowed from ice caps down the valleys and spilled onto the plains. A glacier extended 50 miles down the Green River Valley to an elevation of 7,700', nearly to the site of U.S. 189/191. It was seven miles wide at the Big Bend. Valley glaciers coalesced on the 10,000' terrace from Boulder Canyon to Big Sandy Opening, forming an ice sheet 1,000' thick.

Glaciation

Signs of past glaciation are everywhere. These signs are of two types: glacial erosion and glacial deposition. A glacier's power to sculpt rock is greatest where the ice is thickest. As a result, canyons were deepened and widened into characteristic U-shaped cross sections: steep walls, level floor. At the head of canyons, glaciers carved semicircular bowls: *cirques*. The Cirque of the Towers is but one of perhaps 100 Wind River cirques. Where cirques were carved into opposite sides of a ridge until they intersected, the result was a narrow, jagged crest. The Wind River's most jagged ridges—Mt. Woodrow Wilson, Mt. Bonneville, the Divide from Block Tower past Shark's Nose and Overhanging Tower to Wolf's Head—represent the convergence of back-to-back cirques.

The pressure of thick, steeply descending ice gouged depressions in the bedrock of cirque floors. When the ice retreated, these depressions became many of the range's high lakes.

The sculpting of cirque headwalls, the gouging of lakes, is cumulative from one glacial episode to another and cannot be used to distinguish or enumerate glacial episodes. Geologists, though, can read much in the chaotically heaped boulders of a *moraine*. In particular they can use moraines to separate periods of glaciation, for each glacial advance deposited terminal moraines at its farthest descent of each valley.

A discussion of the sequence of Wind River glaciations is made more vivid by the nomenclature. At the beginning of this century, geologists had no way to correlate the sequences of moraines they found on fringes of the Rocky Mountains with periods of continental glaciation—ice ages—which had been named Nebraskan, Kansan, Illinoian and Wisconsin. Unable to apply these terms in the Rockies, they needed a local terminology.

Above: *Moraines of the Pinedale age impounded the waters of several large lakes—such as Half Moon Lake, seen here—along the western base of the Wind Rivers.* GEORGE WUERTHNER
Facing page: *A small glacier nestles under Mt. Woodrow Wilson and the Sphinx (center).* BARBARA & MICHAEL PFLAUM

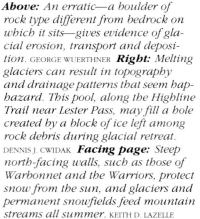

Above: An erratic—a boulder of rock type different from bedrock on which it sits—gives evidence of glacial erosion, transport and deposition. GEORGE WUERTHNER *Right:* Melting glaciers can result in topography and drainage patterns that seem haphazard. This pool, along the Highline Trail near Lester Pass, may fill a hole created by a block of ice left among rock debris during glacial retreat. DENNIS J. CWIDAK *Facing page:* Steep north-facing walls, such as those of Warbonnet and the Warriors, protect snow from the sun, and glaciers and permanent snowfields feed mountain streams all summer. KEITH D. LAZELLE

Eliot Blackwelder, working in western Wyoming in 1915, identified three episodes of Rocky Mountain glaciation. He named each for the locale where he found deposits that he considered to typify an advance. The oldest, which has since been dated at 200,000 years ago, he named the *Buffalo* Glaciation, for the Buffalo Fork of the Snake River, which flows from Togwotee Pass into Jackson Hole. An advance of 140,000 to 50,000 years ago he named the *Bull Lake* Glaciation, because moraines near Bull Lake represented deposition during that period. Professor Blackwelder defined moraines "around each of the large lakes near Pinedale" as type specimens of a glacial advance that climaxed 25,000 years ago and ended 10,000 years ago: thus the *Pinedale* Glaciation. The names Buffalo, Bull Lake and Pinedale were then applied throughout the Rockies and still are in use today.

Each named glacial episode was less extensive than its predecessor. Buffalo moraines were deposited farther from the mountains than Bull Lake moraines, which are in turn farther downvalley than Pinedale moraines. The explanation for this chronological progression is that a glacial advance obliterates most or all evidence of earlier glaciation. If a minor advance is followed by a major advance, the smaller, earlier episode is unlikely to be detected. Presumably, many lesser advances have gone undetected.

Only faint traces of Buffalo glaciation have been found on the fringes of the Wind Rivers. The rubble piles of Bull Lake moraines are notable near the community of Boulder, where the road to Big Sandy Opening leaves U.S. 191, and along this Big Sandy road. Pinedale moraines, toward the southern end of the range, occur from eight to 10 miles downstream from cirque headwalls, at elevations ranging from 8,500' to 9,500'—for example, at Big Sandy Opening. Perhaps the best place to see Pinedale moraines is on the road from Pinedale to Elkhart Park, which climbs a massive morainal ridge and gives a sense of the enormous scale of ice-age glaciation.

Professor Blackwelder's Pinedale moraines impound the waters of Frémont Lake; other large lakes at the western base of the mountains, such as Boulder and Green River lakes, also are dammed by Pinedale moraines. Throughout the range, smaller lakes and ponds lie behind glacial deposits. In the meadows of Big Sandy Opening are randomly scattered, pond-filled depressions that make no sense in terms of stream drainage. These hollows are *kettles* and mark places where a receding glacier dropped a mass of ice among the rock debris; when the ice melted, the resulting hole filled with water. A few Wind River lakes are dammed by rockslides, but most indicate, in one way or the other, past glaciation.

By the end of Pinedale glaciation, the Wind Rivers had been carved into their present form. This last of the ice ages was followed by a warming trend. During the period from 7,500 to 5,000 years ago, known as the *Altithermal* or *Climatic Optimum*, glaciers may have completely disappeared from the Wind Rivers. The glaciers that exist today are not remnants of the ice ages but of more recent minor advances.

While knowledge of the Wind Rivers for the 2 billion years after the granite crystallized can be set forth in a paragraph, the past few thousand years have received much scrutiny. The very recent past, like the oldest rocks and the Laramide uplift, is a subject of current scrutiny. If study of the ancient rocks borders on cosmology, study of glaciation since the ice ages borders on meteorology.

The Altithermal was followed, 5,000 to 3,000 years ago, by renewed, though not extensive, glaciation. The small glaciers, which postdate continental ice sheets, were restricted to higher elevations. In the Rocky Mountains this episode has been called the *Temple Lake* advance; below the north face of Temple Peak lie a small remnant glacier, a series of obvious glacial deposits and moraine-dammed Temple Lake. However, the moraine that inspired the name turned out to represent a minor Pinedale re-advance

Above: *Vivid evidence of glacial action are moraines piled just below the snouts of present glaciers, as here below Dinwoody Glacier.* RON MAMOT
Facing page, left: *Streams continue to shape the land—although the result in the brief period since the ice ages is almost unnoticeable.* JOE KELSEY
Right: *Washakie Glacier, sheltered by the North Face of Bair Peak, is one of the few small glaciers in the southern half of the range. Glaciation is more extensive to the east of the Divide, not only because the northwest-southeast trend of the crest provides more shade on the east, but also because west winds blow snow across the Divide.* GEORGE WUERTHNER

before the Altithermal, and the Temple Lake glaciation has been less-ambiguously renamed *Indian Basin*, for moraines found below Ellingwood Glacier.

Another minor glacial advance occurred from 100 A.D. to 1000 A.D. Its name, *Audubon*, comes from Colorado, not from the Wind Rivers. Audubon deposits occur at 11,000′ in upper Titcomb Basin.

A final set of moraines, lying just below existing glaciers, represent the *Gannett Peak* advance of just 100 to 300 years ago. Geologists date such recent deposits by the absence of soil and vegetation, by the near lack even of lichen. Climbers date them by their instability: the blocks have not had time to settle, and young moraines can be treacherous to cross.

Today

A different kind of evidence also documents the Gannett Peak advance. When Frémont camped by the East Fork River on August 9, 1842, at an elevation below 7,000′, water froze at night. In Indian and Titcomb basins, Frémont found quantities of snow and ice that would shock anyone who has visited these valleys during an August of the 1980s. The southwest slopes of Frémont Peak today are nearly bare during summer, but Frémont describes an August 15 snow line of about 12,000′, which is now typical for June or October.

Today, glaciers survive in the high cirques. A study of Fitzpatrick Wilderness noted "about 30." A study of Popo Agie Wilderness found "a few small glaciers." Distinguishing between true glaciers and merely permanent snowfields was a more important branch of geology in the last century, when John Muir and Clarence King scoured the West for ice that met standards established in the Alps. Today, with drifting, colliding continents to concern them, geologists are less likely to determine whether snow is sufficiently compacted and mobile to qualify as glacial and whether merging glaciers count as one or two.

However, using the arbitrary criterion of being named on topographic maps, it can be said that the Wind Rivers harbor 24 officially named glaciers. The number itself is of little significance, but an analysis of these glaciers reveals a few trends. Of the 24, 22 are in the north, two in the south. Nine are west of the Divide, 15 east.

This second disparity is not accidental. It is due in part to the northwest-southeast trend of the crest; the east side is also the north side and thus shadier than the west side. But the prevailing winds are from the west and east-facing glaciers also owe their survival to snow blown over the Divide. The effect of wind on glaciation is seen most vividly on the west slopes of the westernmost peaks—for example, the Dragon Head-Pronghorn ridge, the Raid-Geikie ridge, Watchtower and Pylon in the Cirque of the Towers, Temple Peak. The west slopes of these peaks apparently escaped ice-age glaciation. While their east faces have been ice-sculpted into near-vertical walls, they are all accessible by scrambling from the "back side."

A further observation that can be made from the map is the consistency with which glaciers end at elevations between

11,100′ and 11,500′. (The lowest-reaching, Grasshopper, ends at 10,900′; the terminus of Frémont Glacier sits in complex terrain at 11,900′.) Between many of these glaciers and their highest terminal moraine sit small ponds. These ponds indicate glacial retreat during the past century.

The largest of the surviving glaciers each occupies roughly one square mile. Three of these flank Gannett Peak; two lie east of the Helen-Frémont ridge. But small as they are compared to former bodies of ice, these glaciers, with scattered rockfall near their heads, rock and gravel mixed with ice in equal measure toward their snouts, lateral moraines and medial moraines where two glaciers flow together, are the best place for appreciating the role of ice in enhancing alpine scenery.

THE HIGHLINE TRAIL

Above: *Most backpackers allow eight to 10 days for the Highline's 64 miles.*
Right: *Sunset at Cook Lakes, near the Highline's midpoint. Evenings find most trekkers camped at one of the many lakes the trail passes.*
DENNIS J. CWIDAK PHOTOS

The Wind River Mountains were pushed up to their present eminence above the plains in intermittent stages. Each pause gave the forces of erosion time to reduce the range's flanks to the level of the plains. When uplift resumed, these peripheral benches, lying on the crystalline core, were raised along with the backbone, resulting—notably on the west side—in a series of steps.

The most prominent of these benches, at elevations ranging from about 10,000' to 10,500', lies below the crest for much of the length of the range. In places the topographic map's 10,000' contour is eight miles from the 10,500' line. It is possible to walk (hundreds each summer do, on one of the range's most popular trails) from Miller Park, overlooking Frémont Lake, to Island Lake, surrounded by 13,000' peaks, without climbing above 10,500' or dropping below 10,000'. You can ascend directly from New Fork Lakes to 10,000', then hike into the heart of the northern Wind Rivers at a nearly constant elevation.

The extent of this terrace perched between the peaks and the plains is a happy circumstance, because it is near treeline—a country of clustered pine and spruce dispersed through broad meadows, of summer wildflowers, of gently cascading and flat, meandering streams and innumerable lakes, ponds, pools and marshes. The feature that most sets the Wind Rivers apart from other ranges, ironically, is this flat west-side upland.

The trail

Paralleling the Wind River crest for 64 miles from Green River Lakes to Big Sandy Opening is a trail that follows this terrace. We call it the Highline Trail, as if one unambiguous path stretched from north to south. In reality, a network of trails traverses the treeline country, and the identity of the Highline is somewhat a matter of terminology. USGS topographic maps and Forest Service signboards have adopted different nomenclature, so a hiker planning a trek from maps and later with a pack on his back sees different Highline Trails. South of Cook Lakes, about midway along the route, the maps label a more easterly, upstream trail "Frémont Trail" and a western, downstream version "Highline Trail." This Frémont Trail, in opener country and nearer the mountains, is also more direct, and

it is the topographers' Frémont Trail that most of us are referring to when we speak of the Highline.

Frémont or Highline, the directness of a trail that parallels the axis of a major mountain chain is remarkable. Such a straightforward upland route along, say, the Tetons or Sierra Nevada is not possible. These ranges are cut crosswise by profound canyons, and traveling north-south in the Tetons or Sierra has the feel of going against the grain. Canyons are not as prominent in the Wind Rivers. None bisects the range, as in the Tetons. There are deep canyons on the west side—notably where Frémont Creek and the New Fork River emerge into foothill lakes, but they are below the 10,000' terrace and have cut back only part way into it. Excepting the Green River itself, which outflanks the terrace by escaping from the range's north end, no west-side stream has eroded back from the plains into the mountains. (East-side streams, such as Dinwoody Creek and the North Popo Agie, do cut continuous canyons from the base of Divide peaks to the valleys; there is not a Highline Trail on the east side.)

The trail over Jackass Pass to the Cirque of the Towers offers views back to the south. East Temple and Temple peaks stand in the distance, Schiestler Peak and Sundance Pinnacle (right) nearer.
CHARLIE CRANGLE

It is the Green's gorge by which the Highline enters the mountains, and the trail along the Green River does not fit the generalities applied to the remainder of the trail. From campground and trailhead on Lower Green River Lake, at 7,961' *the* low point of the route, the Highline traverses the shores of the Green River Lakes, then follows the flat river under Squaretop's massive walls; the bogs here provide a Wind River rarity: moose habitat. At Three Forks Park, 12 miles from the trailhead, the Highline has climbed only to 8,400'.

The next few miles, though, are the most strenuous of the Highline. The three forks cascade down from a thousand or more feet above, and the trail switchbacks beside the western fork, Trail Creek, to Trail Creek Park, where the high country may be said to begin. The scene for the next two miles is typical of Wind River treeline country and is repeated often, with subtle variations, along the Highline. Several-foot–wide Trail Creek—lined with willows, paintbrush, overhanging grass clumps, mimulus and many other flowers—descends a rocky bed through a deep but gently rising linear valley from Green River Pass at 10,362'. Despite its important-sounding name, Green River Pass is an undramatic height-of-land in this long valley, the watershed between north-flowing Trail Creek and the south-flowing headwaters of Pine Creek. So indistinct is the divide that it supports a cluster of ponds; it is hardly obvious which drain north, which drain south.

Unlike classic watershed crests, Green River Pass seems an accident, an afterthought, and the linearity of the trench—the Trail Creek and Pine Creek valleys together—the real topographic feature. In a sense the pass is an afterthought.

Fractures & drainages

Compared to most stream systems, the pattern of Wind River drainage was determined less by streams flowing down the sides of mountains and more by water taking advantage of existing zones of weak rock. These fracture zones are apparently ancient fault lines, existing before the Laramide Revolution of 65 million years ago, existing before the sedimentary layers were deposited. During the Laramide uplift, blocks again moved along these fractures. Movement along faults left linear zones of shattered rock varying in width from 50' or less to one-fourth mile; they

are typically bounded by steep 20′ or 30′ cliffs. Most of these fault-line valleys are occupied by insignificant creeks, some by no creek. It is easier to imagine ice-age glaciers and major streams carving thousand-foot-deep valleys down a slope, perpendicular to the crest, than these secondary trickles eroding the numerous sharp 20′ rifts parallel to the crest, at right angles to the main drainage.

From Green River Pass, the trail follows Pine Creek to isolated Summit Lake. As a rule, the best views in a mountain range are to be had from a peak detached from the main divide. Above Summit Lake rise the low-angle slopes of 12,068′ Glover Peak, a broad massif which as the highest summit west of the entire Highline, offers a panorama of the high peaks, views of peaks far to the south and much

of the west-side country. Much Wind River bedrock is jointed into series of ledges, typically tilted as ramps, and Glover Peak is a good example, with one set of 10′-wide, grass-and-flower-covered ledges sloping up north, another sloping up south. The face above Summit Lake appears difficult because of numerous short cliff bands, but a hiker can turn his/her own zigzagging path into a particularly satisfying ascent.

Pine Creek has cut a sharp little valley into the terrace almost to Summit Lake, and the Highline descends into the trees to cross it before climbing east toward 10,777′ Elbow Lake. The tundra here does little to conceal the pattern of shattered fracture zones. The name Elbow Lake itself suggests the intersection of a fault-line trench with down-

Above: The Highline passes Summit Lake, just south of Green River Pass, in extensive tundra-like meadows. CHARLIE CRANGLE

Left: A scramble up Stroud Peak from Elbow Lake by means of its Southeast Ridge (the right skyline in this view) is one of the most rewarding side trips from the Highline. CHARLIE CRANGLE

Facing page: Perhaps the feature that most distinguishes the Wind Rivers from other ranges is the extensive terrace west of the crest, near treeline. PAT O'HARA

slope drainage, which is indeed the case. Beyond Elbow Lake the trail turns north through an 11,040′ saddle separating Pine Creek waters from those of Frémont Creek. Here the grassy south slopes of 12,198′ Stroud Peak tempt a hiker to another of the Wind Rivers' most pleasant easy ascents.

Upper and Lower Jean lakes are long and thin, stretching from northwest to southeast, as are numerous fault-line lakes whose shores the Highline follows. Frémont Creek emerges from Lower Jean Lake and flows southeast to Island Lake, but through a defile unsuited for horses and backpackers. The creek, however, emerges from Island Lake flowing west, and the Highline meets it again at a bridge dignified with a name: Frémont Crossing.

In the next two miles, drainage seems chaotic—ponds in unlikely hollows, streams running in unexpected direc-

tions. One senses hacked topography: fault fractures, again. The trail's zigzagging through these nicks ends near Little Seneca Lake, a major intersection where the Highline crosses the well-traveled Island Lake Trail.

The Highline is never quite in the mountains, for the terrace does not abut directly against alpine faces, nor do glaciers any longer extend out onto the terrace. However, in several places along the range, especially where the scenery is most impressive, ice-age glaciers did carve low-gradient valleys back into the mountains, typically ending in cirque headwalls. Glacial scouring was intense at the bottom of these bowls, and beneath the headwalls lie the best-known lakes. These lakes are typically a jaunt of a few miles by a trail that crosses the Highline (though the rugged two miles from Little Seneca Lake to Island Lake is a strenuous jaunt), and most Highline trekkers make occasional side trips farther into the mountains.

The lakes region

From Little Seneca Lake can be seen hard work ahead on the Highline; for two miles it climbs a straight, open valley to the trail's high point, 11,080′ Lester Pass. Beyond Lester Pass, where the character of the terrain changes from rocky and grandiose to gentler, opener, more serene, the trail passes just out of sight of the large Cook Lakes.

At Cook Lakes' outlet stream, Pole Creek, nomenclatural ambiguity begins. The Highline proper begins a long detour by descending Pole Creek for two miles to 9,720′ Pole Creek Lakes. Again turning southeast, for nine miles to the outlet of North Fork Lake, it traverses country below 10,000′. To compensate for the lack of alpine scenery, the Highline follows the shores of numerous lakes—the Chain Lakes, Barnes Lake, Horseshoe Lake, Lake George—for much of this distance. The Frémont Trail takes a more direct route, climbing into the pond-filled tundra of Bald Mountain Basin and, continuing above treeline, crossing several ridges en route to the inlet of North Fork Lake.

South of North Fork Lake the character of the terrain again subtly changes. The land is slightly lower and less barren. The Frémont Trail now follows a fault line past many small lakes; the Highline, a mile or so to the west, wanders from lake to lake in more amorphous, less linear terrain. Cross trails follow the Middle Fork of Boulder Creek to its head at one of the larger high lakes, half-mile-long, 10,252′-high Middle Fork Lake.

Both trails enter the two-by-five-mile, gently rolling meadow through which are scattered sizeable lakes: Bob's, Dream, Raid, South Fork, Crescent and Cross. Nearly from the meadow rise the low-angle grass-and-talus slopes of Dragon Head and Pronghorn, of Raid, Ambush and Geikie—west-facing slopes from which, apparently, enough ice-age snow was blown to prevent glacial sculpting. The Highline offers glimpses beyond these unprepossessing hulks, and a hiker may be tempted into a side trip. In particular, the walls, spires and arêtes of Mt. Bonneville, above the valley where the South Fork of Boulder Creek cuts between the Dragon Head-Pronghorn and Raid-Geikie ridges, is in sight from much of the meadow. The gentle-sloped peaks, promising outstanding views without technical difficulty, are also popular diversions for Highline trekkers.

Above: Water lilies on one of the many ponds passed by the Highline. DENNIS J. CWIDAK

Left: Extensive treeline meadows are a boon to flowers, such as these yellow composites and purple polemoniums, which the poetic call sky pilots and the overly-sensitive call skunkflowers. CHARLIE CRANGLE

The Highline ends at Big Sandy Opening, but hikers wishing to continue south can go on past Big Sandy Lake, Schiestler Peak (right) and over the pass left of Temple Peak (background). PAT O'HARA

South of Mt. Geikie, the East Fork River emerges from a flat, grassy-floored valley walled by 1,800′ cliffs. In the stretch where the Frémont/Highline crosses it, the East Fork is a classic mountain stream, not of the tumultuous type but gliding down bedrock slabs and over a boulder-lined bed. Maps show no trail leading up the East Fork, but none is needed; the going is easy, well-used, and the way hard to lose.

The Frémont/Highline crosses the East Fork where Washakie Creek joins it. Toward the head of this creek can be seen one of the Wind Rivers' distinctive scenes: the uniquely serrated crest of the Cirque of the Towers, seen from "the back." A trail ascends Washakie Creek's open valley for three miles to 10,287′ Shadow Lake, above which loom Overhanging Tower and Shark's Nose.

These Cirque summits are often in sight during the final miles of the Frémont/Highline as it passes Marm's Lake, Dad's Lake and another extensive park called Fish Creek Meadows, before entering woods and dropping anticlimactically to the Big Sandy River and the Big Sandy Opening Trailhead.

Off the beaten path

The Wind Rivers by definition extend from Togwotee Pass to South Pass. Nearly all of the scenery of note lies between Green River Lakes and Big Sandy Opening, and that the Highline Trail parallels only half of the range is a startling realization. Maps do indicate a Highline Trail heading north from Green River Lakes to Union Pass, but few hikers are aware of this seldom-used path, and touching civilization at Green River Lakes detracts from the continuous back-country ambience of the 64 miles south of Green River Lakes.

Energetic backpackers, however, sometimes continue south from Big Sandy Opening. The most scenic route involves the much-traveled thoroughfare to Big Sandy Lake, then a trail that climbs south past Clear and Deep lakes and through the 11,500′ pass between Temple and East Temple peaks and descends yet another open, gentle, steep-walled valley, that of Little Sandy Creek. The west-side possibilities beyond Little Sandy Lake are relatively unattractive; perhaps the best strategy is to cross the Divide by 10,327′ Sweetwater Gap, then descend the Middle

Ironically, trails are difficult to follow across this vast meadow. The going is easy, so trails have not been constructed and maintained; humanity, not constrained to a narrow path, has not worn one. Cairns mark the formal trails, but cairns mark informal routes as well, sheepherders have whiled away time creating elaborate cairn–sculptures, and rock piles have sprouted for no apparent reason. With unmistakable Mt. Bonneville for a landmark and lakes sprawled in distinctive cookie-cutter shapes, a topographic map is especially useful, even if the trail it names Highline wanders off to low country, while backpackers refer to the more interesting Frémont Trail as the Highline.

Popo Agie for 16 miles from its headwaters to its 7,139′ trailhead—the lowest in the Wind Rivers—near Sinks Canyon and Lander. The Middle Popo Agie drops the 3,000′ through varying terrain, cascading over rocks, meandering through marshes, running quietly but powerfully down straight channels. Wind River Peak and its several east-side cirques dominate the alpine scenery, while a hiker who is emerging from the high country is shocked by the sight of bitterroot, prickly pear and other arid-land vegetation.

A still more adventurous scheme for hiking the length of the Wind Rivers involves paralleling the crest higher than the Highline. Such a route involves much trailless hiking, but with open, linear valleys and tundra, the way is seldom

difficult. Much of the pleasure of such an undertaking is in laying out maps and devising a higher-than-Highline route; let it suffice to say that at the south end one notes the possibility of entering the Cirque of the Towers by Jackass Pass and leaving by Texas Pass, of ascending the East Fork Valley for five easy miles and crossing the pass between Bonneville and Raid and quickly crossing another pass to Middle Fork Lake. In the northern Wind Rivers, Knapsack Col, which connects Peak Lake's alpine valley with Titcomb Basin, and the flower-sloped, gentle, but nameless saddle between Island Lake and Wall Lake are likely to be key elements. A route could be chosen, not by studying a trail map, but by means of a geological map that indicates fault lines.

Above: On the popular backpack from the Elkhart Park trailhead to Island Lake, the high peaks come into view near Seneca Lake. Frémont Peak is on the left, Jackson Peak center, and Ellingwood Peak right. Just left of the dead snag, a bit of Little Seneca Lake can be seen; here the Island Lake Trail crosses the Highline. PAT O'HARA

Left: Near the southeast corner of the range, the Popo Agie emerges from the mountains in Sinks Canyon, just above Lander. KENT & DONNA DANNEN

VEGETATION

Above: *The columbine might be called one of the symbols of the Wind River Range.* PAT O'HARA

Right: *Wind River forests form a belt—above the plains, below tree-line. Seen here, the Green River just below Green River Lakes.* M. VIDAK

Facing page, top: *Aspen groves, typically found from 8,200' to 9,200', support a lush, varied understory.* LARRY ULRICH

Bottom: *This avens species is called prairie smoke or old man's whiskers.* PAT O'HARA

When Washakie, during the 1860s, was negotiating for a reservation for his Shoshones, one of the attractions of the Wind River valley was its proximity to forests. Few trees grew to the east and south; wood was a valuable commodity to a Plains tribe. The forest belt that circles the Wind River chain stands out darkly in contrast both to the vast sagebrush plains from which the mountains rise and to the tundra, bedrock, talus and glaciers above treeline. Robert M. Reed identified six forest types in this zone that extends from approximately 7,500'-8,000' to 10,200'-10,500'.

Many factors determine what vegetation grows at a particular site, but two factors—altitude and moisture—tend to be most important in characterizing a habitat. Although ecological considerations are more complex, assigning the six forest types to niches determined by these two factors gives a general idea of the distribution of plants in the Wind Rivers. The wetness or dryness of a habitat is in turn dependent on the direction in which it slopes—shaded north slopes tending to be wetter than sunny south slopes, windward west slopes to be drier than leeward east slopes.

Drier habitats near the lower margin of the forest—particularly from 8,200' to 9,200'—support numerous stands of quaking aspen *(Populus tremuloides),* one of the scenic attractions of the Rocky Mountains. While in much of the West aspens are an intermediate step in a vegetation cycle—a seral forest type—and will eventually be replaced by conifers, Reed found in the Wind Rivers "no signs of successful conifer invasion of the sites," that the aspen stands "appear to be relatively stable communities."

Aspens are but one element—the overstory—of a complex plant community. Beneath the aspens is a notably lush understory of shrubs, grasses and other herbaceous plants. Wind River aspen communities are characterized by three shrub species: snowberry *(Symphoricarpos oreophilus),* Oregon grape *(Berberis repens)* and wild rose *(Rosa woodsii).* The herbaceous layer is characterized by the flowering plants yarrow *(Achillea millefolium),* elegant aster *(Aster perelegans),* Richardson's geranium *(Geranium richardsoni),* lodgepole lupine *(Lupinus argenteus)* and cinquefoil *(Potentilla gracilis).* Aspen stands that have been heavily grazed by sheep and cattle, as much of the Wind

Rivers' low country has, support a slightly different understory. Snowberry, otherwise the most characteristic shrub, may be absent, being replaced by bearberry *(Arctostaphyllos uva-ursi),* juniper *(Juniperus communis),* green gentian *(Frasera speciosa)* and dandelions *(Taraxacum sp.).*

Aspens are occasionally found above 10,000', but only in small pockets on talus slopes with little soil and without the characteristic undergrowth.

Forests in which Douglas fir *(Pseudotsuga menziesii)* predominate occur generally between 7,200' and 8,500', just above the sagebrush but on north-facing slopes (a moister habitat than that of aspens). Mixed with the Douglas firs are typically a few lodgepole pines *(Pinus contorta)* and limber pines *(P. flexilis).* The shrubs that dominate the thick understory of the Douglas fir forests are snowberry, Oregon grape and juniper. In young stands, less shady than mature stands, Rocky Mountain maple *(Acer glabrum)* and serviceberry *(Amelanchier alnifolia)*

Clockwise from above: *Silky phacelia, one of the common flowers of high meadows.* ERWIN & PEGGY BAUER
The cone of a whitebark pine, one of the dominant treeline conifers.
W. PERRY CONWAY
This whitebark pine has withstood many a storm. GEORGE WUERTHNER
The bright color of Parry's primrose is often a startling contrast to that of its rocky habitat. JOE KELSEY
The Wind Rivers support a number of species in the sunflower family.
PAT O'HARA

48

Clockwise from left: *Monkey flowers.* JOE KELSEY
Glacier lilies appear early in summer soon after snow melts. KENNAN WARD
Thistles bloom later in summer than most flowering plants. PAT O'HARA
Marsh marigolds prefer wet ground, as in this Cirque of the Towers meadow. The peaks are, from left to right, Watchtower, Block Tower, Shark's Nose, Overhanging Tower, Wolf's Head and Pingora. JEFF GNASS

49

Above: Whitebark pine. JOHN McCONNELL
Top: This blossom, understandably, is known as "butter and eggs."
KENNAN WARD
Right: Wood does not decay rapidly in a dry, cold climate. The size of this ancient specimen compared to the Cirque of the Towers' present dwarfed treeline conifers suggests more favorable conditions, perhaps before the Gannett Peak glacial advance of 100 to 300 years ago. The peaks are, left to right: Pylon, South Watchtower, Watchtower, Block Tower, Shark's and Overhanging Tower. JEFF GNASS

particular flower species is the bluegrass species, *Poa nervosa.*

Also at intermediate elevations, with some preference for moist, north-facing slopes, are forests of subalpine fir *(Abies lasiocarpa)* mixed with Engelmann spruce *(Picea engelmanni)* and lodgepole pine. The distinction between these mixed forests and purer lodgepole stands is blurred by lodgepole's tendency to return before fir and spruce on burned or logged slopes, but this mixed-conifer community can be distinguished from others by the dominant shrubs—wintergreen *(Pyrola secunda)*, currant *(Ribes montigenum)*, Buffalo berry, whortleberry *(Vaccinium scoparium*, a huckleberry species with small, exquisite-tasting reddish berries)—and flowering plants—columbine *(Aquilegia coerulea)*, lodgepole lupine, goldenrod *(Solidago multiradiata)* and western meadowrue *(Thalictrum occidentale).*

Between 9,500′ and timberline are stands dominated by whitebark pine *(Pinus albicaulis)* and the similarly five-needled limber pine. These usually small stands do not support the dense understory that lower habitats do; whortleberry, arnica and bluegrass compete with rock outcrops and thick accumulations of pine needles as ground cover.

Also above 9,500′, but typically on moister slopes than the whitebark-limber pine stands, are forests of Engelmann spruce, with a small representation of subalpine fir and lodgepole pine. Again, the understory is dominated by whortleberry. The only regularly present flowering plants are heart-leaved arnica and fireweed *(Epibolium angustifolium)*, as colder temperatures and a shorter growing season restrict the number of plants that can grow at this elevation. Nevertheless, trees in this zone tend to be larger than at lower elevations, a fact that may be attributed to space between trees or, at least until the past few decades, distance from humanity.

One species of tree is conspicuous by its absence from the Wind Rivers (and from the Tetons, Absarokas and Gros Ventres): ponderosa pine, which is prominently represented in most mountain forests of the American West.

are also common shrubs. As for herbaceous plants, grasses are more prominent than flowering plants, heart-leaved arnica *(Arnica cordifolia)* being the one conspicuous wildflower in the shade of Douglas firs.

Relatively dry slopes and flats above aspen habitat but not extending as high as treeline—between 7,900′ and 9,500′—are typically forested with lodgepole pine, especially in the southern Wind Rivers. Lodgepole forests occur in conjunction with an understory in which juniper and Buffalo berry *(Shepherdia canadensis)* are the common shrubs. Reed found a variety of flowering plants in the lodgepole stands he studied, mentioning three in particular: milk vetch *(Astragalus miser)*, yarrow and pale agoseris *(Agoseris glauca)*. More characteristic of lodgepole forests than any

Timberline

Ecologists prefer to define timberline without wind being a factor, but in the Wind Rivers this situation is so theoretical that no one has determined an idealized, windless elevation. Actual timberline is roughly 10,500′—give or take a few hundred feet for exposed west slopes and sheltered east slopes.

Timberline, of course, is not a distinct line, and scattered representatives of coniferous species survive above the zone where forests predominate. Near treeline are Engelmann spruce, subalpine fir and whitebark pine, but at the upper limit of isolated trees, spruce alone grows tall enough to be considered a tree.

Trees above timberline are of particular interest, both scenically and in their adaptation to a marginal environment. Wind-blown ice inhibits the growth of needles and branches on the windward side, so the trees take on an asymmetrical aspect, appearing to be wind-buffeted even in calm weather. Most characteristic of tree life above timberline is *krummholz,* crooked-wood—low, huddled, twisted coniferous masses. Snow drifts protect lower branches from storms, but ice particles blast and destroy parts of the tree that protrude from the snow. (Protruding trees may be further damaged by animals gnawing on bark when other food is snow-covered.)

Branches of subalpine fir in particular, but also Engelmann spruce, can take root where they touch the ground, as they may when bowed down by snow. Branches near these second-generation roots may become trunk-like, and branches from these trunks may themselves take root, so a single plant comes to look like a clump of small trees. When the original trunk dies off a mysteriously hollow circle of fir or spruce remains.

One of the nobler spectacles above timberline is a large, isolated spruce. These trees have a look about them of having withstood many storms, as indeed they have. Many, at least, are relics of a time, before the Gannett Peak glacial advance of 100 to 300 years ago, when the climate was warmer than now and trees could thus thrive at higher elevations. A hiker at Big Sandy Opening who had just completed the Highline Trail was once asked what the most unforgettable sight along the way was. His response was unexpected: large, ancient trees along the 10,500′ to 10,800′ stretch of trail between Bald Mountain Basin and North Fork Lake.

Left to right: Lichens on sedimentary rock. W. PERRY CONWAY *Berries of mountain ash.* ERWIN A. BAUER *Alpine laurel, or swamp laurel.* PAT O'HARA

51

WILDLIFE

Above: *Mule deer.* ED WOLFF
Right: *The best moose habitat in the
Wind Rivers is along the upper Green
River.* ERWIN & PEGGY BAUER

On maps, northwestern Wyoming appears segmented by boundary lines—accentuated by colors indicating administrative areas—into Yellowstone National Park, Grand Teton National Park, Shoshone, Bridger-Teton and Targhee national forests (which are further segmented into wilderness areas and primitive areas), an Indian reservation, a national elk refuge. Wyoming itself is separated by more conspicuous, straighter lines from Montana and Idaho. *Homo sapiens* is the only species to see these lines, however, and most of northwestern Wyoming and parts of the adjacent states are in fact a single wildlife preserve.

Human impacts

Maps of now-industrialized states sometimes make one pause to wonder why certain communities were named for certain animals—Buffalo, New York, for instance; Beaver Falls and Elk Grove, Pennsylvania. Creatures that once roamed much of America have become concentrated in the Wyoming mountains. For many species this area is a last refuge—for grizzly bears, bison, bald eagles, trumpeter swans, for black-footed ferrets. For most species these mountains are part of their former range, but a few—moose, coyote—are not native but have migrated here to escape human pressure elsewhere.

Yet, while this high country may approximate primeval wilderness, the presence of whites during the past two centuries has affected wildlife more than is apparent to a 20th-century backpacker. An archaeologist notes that the Buffalo Fork of the Snake, flowing west from Togwotee Pass, was well-named. Astorians, in 1811, found grizzly bears in the Wind River Valley and crossed Union Pass to find "herds of buffalo quietly grazing" on the Green River. Frémont, in 1842, found pronghorn in the Wind Rivers above Boulder Lake and signs of beavers nearly to Pole Creek Lake. Returning from the climb of his peak, he found "large flocks" of bighorn sheep below Island Lake. Hayden Surveyors, in 1877, saw 100 bighorn sheep on Wind River Peak and a grizzly bear on the Big Sandy. A Wind River visitor will not see these species in these places today. Coyotes have prospered in the Wind Rivers because of the elimination of wolves and mountain lions.

Nevertheless, the present wildlife population is not a still-dwindling remnant of the pre-Lewis-and-Clark population. Just as today's glaciers represent a bit of a comeback from the near-disappearance of glaciers during the Altithermal of 7,500 to 5,000 years ago, the animals that presently make the Wyoming mountains home represent a comeback from a low point around 1900, when human pressures were maximum and conservation efforts minimal. The increase in wildlife during this century, in fact, has required the active cooperation of humanity.

While the Wind River high country has not changed significantly, many species seen in the mountains during summer—the large ungulates in particular—move downhill in winter. It is man's presence in the valleys that has most affected wildlife. Ranching deprived elk of winter forage and forced them from ancient migratory routes through the intermontane valleys. Bighorn sheep have prospered in the northern Wind Rivers only after being given winter feeding

Coyotes have adapted well to the mountains in the few centuries since human pressures forced them from the low country. MICHAEL S. QUINTON

grounds in the Wind River Valley. Mobile pronghorn antelope are horribly vulnerable to fences.

That a variety of creatures inhabit the Wyoming mountains does not mean they share a single habitat. A 1975 Wyoming Game and Fish Department report estimated the number of big game animals in the administrative districts that comprise the Wind Rivers, Gros Ventres, Tetons, Wyoming Range, much of the Absarokas, and the adjacent valleys. The estimates were 15,750 pronghorn antelope, 30,500 mule deer, ·31,200 elk, 6,100 moose, 725 bighorn sheep and 1,150 black bears. These creatures are by no means evenly distributed throughout the various mountain habitats. While the estimates were not broken down by mountain range, the Wind Rivers are home to few of these

moose and bears, which prefer wetter, lusher habitat, while supporting a disproportionate share of bighorns and pronghorns, which thrive in dry, open country.

In the Wind Rivers, four ungulates—neglecting the more adaptable mule deer—essentially divide up the summer habitats. Pronghorn antelope occupy the plains below the forests, moose the swampy river bottoms (of which the Wind Rivers have few), elk the alpine meadows and sparsely forested slopes near treeline, and bighorn sheep the tundras above timberline. Grizzlies have not been reported for many years. Black bears often make a living in the Green River Lakes Campground, but if one is encountered elsewhere, it is news that travels through the backpacking grapevine.

If an animal were chosen as the emblem of the Wind Rivers, it would be the bighorn sheep. Bighorns have found ideal summer habitat on the vast planar surfaces, far above treeline, at the range's north end.

MARK NEWMAN; TOM STACK & ASSOCIATES

Bighorn Sheep

A Wyoming Game and Fish Department bulletin reports: "Typical bighorn terrain is made up of sheer and broken rim rocks which command a good view of the surrounding country." North of the Wind Rivers' high peaks, between the upper Green River on the west side and the town of Dubois in the upper Wind River Valley, are 100 square miles of such terrain.

Among the physiological advantages that bighorn have in this open, barren country are good eyesight and a low requirement for water. Observers have noted sheep going three days without visiting a stream, and during winter they get what water they need from snow.

The bighorns that roam the high erosion surfaces and gently dipping strata of the northern Wind Rivers are known as the Whiskey Mountain herd. Whiskey Mountain is a summit, east of the Divide, on whose slopes the sheep tend to concentrate. From Whiskey Mountain both the more extensive Divide plateaus, such as Ram Flat, and winter grounds in the Wind River Valley are easily accessible. (One of the other plateaus is named Goat Flat, but there are no mountain goats in the Wind Rivers.)

Whiskey Mountain is one of the best and best-known sheep habitats in the United States. During the 1950s, it supported 400 to 500 sheep; in 1976, the number had risen to 850 to 900. The increase was due in part to the acquisition of winter range in the valley, near Dubois, even if overgrazing is a limiting factor, with elk and domestic cattle grazing much of the same land.

Despite hunting, the population continues to increase, and sheep have been transplanted to other ranges of Wyoming, Nevada, Utah, New Mexico and South Dakota. Between 1949 and 1976, 875 sheep were transplanted—that is, the resident population and the transplanted population were about the same.

Bighorns' relation to mankind involves a paradox that both biologists and Wind River wanderers have noted. During the 1960s bighorns were often seen near the Cirque of the Towers. Now, with more people visiting such places as the Cirque, sheep are rarely seen south of Downs' Mountain. The plateaus north of Downs' Mountain see as little human traffic as any place in the lower 48. As an overall pattern, a bighorn population does not thrive near people. However, the sheep are curious enough about people to often seem tame. One group quickly learned to approach a biologist to lick salt he held out to them. A hiker on Whiskey Mountain found himself being watched, from a short distance away, by a dozen bighorns who had apparently come to see a man lose his temper at his dogs for chasing bighorns.

Beavers

Various sources of hoped-for wealth have lured Americans west. The particular commodity that first drew white men to the Wind Rivers was the largest North American rodent. It was the beaver's misfortune to have barbed fur that pressed well into felt.

The pre-Columbian beaver population of North America has been estimated at 60 million. Cartier in 1535 found Indians in the Gulf of St. Lawrence trading beaver fur to European fishermen. Within a century, the French had to search inland for fur. By 1830 the Wind Rivers were the heart of the richest fur country remaining. By 1900 only a small remnant beaver population survived in the West. During the 20th century, however, with minimal trapping and efforts to preserve and restore habitat, beavers have made something of a comeback. Trapping was prohibited in Wyoming from 1899 to 1919. A 1952 survey of the U.S. and Canada compiled estimates that totaled somewhat more than 1 million beavers, even if the species occupies only one third of its former range. The estimate for Wyoming was 60,000.

Beavers have distinct food preferences; aspen is first, followed by willow, cottonwood, alder and birch. They will sample about anything, but the correlation between the presence of aspen and the presence of beavers is strong. In the Wind Rivers aspens range from the first step that rises from the Green River and Wind River basins, at about 7,500', to the lower edge of the meadows on the 10,000' terrace. Most trailheads lie within this elevation range, and around New Fork Lake for instance, around Boulder Lake, and a few miles below Big Sandy Opening, where the road crosses Dutch Joe Creek, the work of beavers is much in evidence. A beaver's work is more likely to be seen than the beaver itself, for they are mainly nocturnal.

The work, of course, consists of dams, underwater lodges, pondside burrows, small mounds of sticks and mud and tree stumps with obvious tooth marks. They use the food plants as construction materials, but use other woody plants as well, including conifers.

One beaver may fell 200 to 300 trees, up to two feet in diameter, a year. Beavers are credited with intentionally cutting trees to fall toward a pond, but beaver-felled trees can

Above: Beavers were intimately associated with the history of white man in the Wind River and Green River valleys. However, now protected, they thrive at elevations where aspens are prevalent. A beaver spends much time grooming, in order to waterproof its fur.
ALAN D. BRIERE; TOM STACK & ASSOCIATES
Left: A beaver rarely is found far from water.
GARY RANDALL; TOM STACK & ASSOCIATES

Beavers, largely nocturnal, are seen less often than their work. A beaver dam and the pond it forms have a profound effect on the landscape, creating habitat for numerous other aquatic species.
JACK D. SWENSON; TOM STACK & ASSOCIATES

Facing page, left: *White man's presence in the West during the past 20 years has affected the fauna even of mountain wilderness. Trappers in the early 19th century regularly encountered mountain lions, but a sighting today would be a note-worthy event.* ED WOLFF

Right: *One of the finest sights in the Wind Rivers is that of a golden eagle soaring high along a cliff face in early evening.* KENNAN WARD

be seen lying randomly, and if a disproportionate number do fall pondward, there is a simple explanation. Trees standing on a shore have more space and sunlight for growing branches on the lakeward or streamward side, so a tree more often than not is weighted to topple as the beaver would want—into the water. Falling trees are an occasional source of beaver mortality.

A beaver uses its flat, stiff tail as a rudder while it swims and slaps the water with it to warn other beavers of danger, but the tail also serves as a third point of support when a beaver stands on its hind legs to gird a tree with its sharp front incisors. This is one of several anatomical adaptions that make possible a beaver's complicated work. The front paws are human-like—a beaver eating bark has been likened to a person eating corn on the cob—making it possible to carry sticks while swimming, the webbed rear paws doing the paddling. A beaver's lips close behind its front incisors.

Despite these adaptations and a beaver's clumsiness on land, it does not spend as much time in water as might be imagined. On the contrary, it takes special pains to keep itself and its den as dry as possible, shaking itself when it leaves the water, grooming its fur with a waterproofing oil that it secretes.

While a dammed pond is the most obvious sign of beavers, it is not a necessity. What is necessary is still water deep enough to remain unfrozen in winter. Flat stretches of larger streams can serve this purpose. If a lake is already suitable for a beaver's needs, it does not try to improve the pond, but if the pond is not suitable, it builds a dam before making a home. Beavers must also repair dams.

The lodge, built of sticks and plastered with mud, is near the edge of a pond or stream. In the floor are two or more tunnels that connect with the bank. However, not all beavers live in lodges: some live in pondside or streamside burrows. A lodge protects a beaver from all predators but otters.

Of simpler construction are scent mounds, amorphous piles of stick and mud, perhaps two feet around. Beavers mark territory with castoreum, the secretion of special scent glands. It was the musky smell of castoreum used as bait that proved the beaver's undoing when white trappers came west.

Beavers store saplings and sticks underwater for winter, by weighting them with mud or catching them under snags.

A beaver colony typically consists of a mating pair, a litter of kits and yearlings from the previous year's litter. Breeding occurs in February; the young are born in June. Two-year-olds either leave the colony or are driven away; they then establish their own colony.

A young beaver typically makes a new home within a few miles upstream or downstream, but hard-to-imagine cross-country treks have been documented. One short-lived experiment resulted in a dam, made from willows, across a stream at 10,500' in the Cirque of the Towers. A pond flooded several acres of meadow, but the dam did not survive a winter.

Pikas

Except for Sweetwater Gap, at the head of the Sweetwater River, the Wind River crest is above treeline from Union Peak nearly to Pabst Peak, a linear distance of 75 miles. The average width of this alpine band is five or six miles. Some of this zone is covered with permanent snow, some is bedrock, but much is talus and much supports alpine and tundra-like vegetation. Talus and rockslides near and above treeline are home to the small mammal called the pika *(Ochotona princeps)*. (Pikas are also commonly but incorrectly called "conies"; true conies are an Asian and African species that is not closely related.)

Pikas are members of the same order as rabbits (Lago-morphs), although their most obvious features bear small resemblance to what we think of as rabbit features (and contribute to the misconception of pikas as rodents). Pikas are smaller than any rabbit (6″-8″ long). Their ears are small and round, more like Mickey Mouse's than the long ears of a rabbit. Pikas' hind legs are scarcely longer than

their front legs, again in contrast to rabbits. And pikas' tails are so short as to appear to be lacking.

Rabbits are noted for their silence, while what is likely to draw one's attention to a pika is its vocal activity, a series of short sounds that have been described as "squeaks," "bleats," "barks," and "meows." Frémont at Island Lake, hearing his first pika, thought he was hearing a young sheep. Today above 10,000′, though, a pika's cries could be mistaken only for those of a marmot, which one soon recognizes as more whistle-like.

Were it not for the bleats, pikas would rarely be noticed by hiking humanity, for their gray-to-brown coats blend well with the rocks. Not only are talus slopes and rockslides essential to a pika; the crevices among the rocks must be of the proper size. The crevices must be large enough to admit a pika but too small for larger predators. The bleats are made by a sentinel perched on a large rock that offers a wide view and that slopes back toward the hillside. The sentinel warns the pika colony of coyotes, pine martens, hawks, falcons and other birds of prey. The cries also warn marmots and squirrels of predators, but the marmot reciprocates: a marmot's whistle alerts pikas to danger. When a pika sentinel spies a weasel, however, discretion becomes the better part of valor, and it silently retreats into the rocks. A passing climber is large enough that the pika barks rather than retreats.

In large talus fields, pikas tend to live near the edges—close to food. They seem to eat nearly any available plant—such high-elevation shrubs as dwarf huckleberry, raspberry, snowberry, Oregon grape and twinflower; such flowering herbaceous plants as lupines, vetches, alpine sunflower and buckwheats; and conifer twigs. Pikas receive minimal competition for food from other species. Of the other small mammals that share a pika's habitat, marmots range much farther from rocks (and are far less shy about visiting backpackers' camps) and golden–mantled squirrels are seed eaters.

The pika's diet is of particular interest (and particularly accessible to study) because of a unique adaptation to alpine life. Unlike other mountain mammals, the pika neither migrates to low country during winter nor hibernates. In addition to thick, soft fur and furry feet, a pika needs a winter's food supply. Thus one of the most startling sights in otherwise desolate, isolated tundra far from treeline, or on the grassy ledges that cut even the steepest rock walls: miniature "hay piles." A pika begins storing herbs and shrubs in early summer; by early autumn building hay piles is its main activity. Some piles are under rock, but more often they are in the open, where, presumably, the hay is sun-cured. Pikas' hay piles may grow to be as much as two feet high; some pikas build one pile, while others work on several simultaneously.

While pikas live in loose colonies, each animal claims a territory in the rocks and chases out intruders (although feeding grounds often overlap). One study of favorable terrain found about five pikas per acre. Much of the barking is not an altruistic sentinel warning a colony but one pika defending his territory from another. The sexes of the intruder and of the defender seem to make no difference. Territorial defense is most aggressive in autumn, when food gathering is also most frenetic.

To many, the Wind Rivers are synonymous with trout—cutthroat, rainbow, golden, brown, brook—even if fish are not always as abundant as these trout in the Middle Popo Agie in Sinks Canyon State Park, near Lander
KENT & DONNA DANNEN

How pikas spend the winter, in rock dens beneath the snow, is an intriguing mystery that science has felt little compelled to explore. They construct tunnels through the snow, and they occasionally bark. Perhaps they must defend their hay against such intruders as mice and woodrats, but perhaps they occasionally venture out for food other than their hay piles.

No more is known about pikas' courtship behavior than is known about their winter life, except that during breeding season, May and early June, they become less territorial toward the opposite sex. After a 30-day gestation period, a female gives birth to a litter of two to four. The short alpine summer imposes a tight schedule on pika young. A late spring can wipe out a litter. The young can walk in eight days, and reach full size after 40 or 50 days; a pika must grow up quickly, because by the end of the short alpine summer it must have established territory and stored hay. A female can bear a second litter in early July, in preparation for which she drives the first litter from her home.

HISTORY

Above: *Douglas fir.*
THOMAS KITCHIN; TOM STACK & ASSOCIATES
Right: *"Island Lake, Wind River Range, Wyoming," by Albert Bierstadt. Frémont's 1842 party camped by these same falls, which drop into Island Lake from Titcomb Basin.* BUFFALO BILL HISTORICAL CENTER
Facing page: *The Sieur de la Verendrye's dream of reaching the Western Sea was thwarted by an unsympathetic French government, but his sons may have reached the Wyoming Rockies, possibly having been the first whites to see the Wind Rivers.* WYOMING STATE ARCHIVES, MUSEUMS AND HISTORICAL DEPARTMENT

As the last Pleistocene ice sheet began retreating 15,000 to 12,000 years ago, an ice-free corridor apparently opened east of the Rockies. This was at the time that nomadic tribes, having recently crossed the Bering land bridge from Asia to Alaska, were spreading through North America, so man may have discovered South Pass early in his days on this continent. Beautiful Yuma points, knives and scrapers dated at 7,000 to 9,000 years old have been found at Eden, near the junction of the Big Sandy River and Little Sandy Creek, 30 miles southwest of the pass. Someone, or his prey, left a Yuma point just under the Divide in the northern Wind Rivers.

The concept of discovery is clearer in the abstract than when applied to the history of a specific place, and the concept applied to humanity's association with the Wind Rivers is fuzzier than in most places. As always, there is the problem of descendants of Europeans discovering land that had been inhabited, in the case of the Wind Rivers, perhaps 9,000 years ago. Beyond this perennial problem, though, are questions of what early visitors thought they saw, what we think they saw, and what those who followed them by a few years knew of their explorations. Despite this disclaimer, though perhaps because of it, it must be said that the Wind Rivers have a colorful history of discovery.

Explorers & trappers

One of the heartbreaking sagas of American exploration is that of the Sieur de la Verendrye. Verendrye's consuming ambition was to cross the continent to the Western Sea, but the French government insisted he finance his explorations through fur trading, then denied him his profits and requested more furs. Verendrye, a native of Quebec, first went west in 1728. By 1734 he had built a post at Lake Winnipeg; in 1738 he reached the Missouri River in North Dakota. Trade and Indian wars kept him from exploring farther, but in 1742-1743 his two sons made a final effort to reach the Western Sea.

Louis-Joseph and Francois started southwest with a tribe they called the Horse People, but the Horse People

(continued on page 68)

The peak right of center could not have been the summit reached by Benjamin Bonneville—first man known to climb in the Wind Rivers—and why his name was bestowed on it is a mystery. M. VIDAK

Captain Bonneville

The first two reported Wind River climbing parties were led by men whose fathers were victims of French politics. Benjamin Eulalie de Bonneville's father had opposed Napoleon; Bonneville *fils* and his mother came to America. He graduated from West Point in 1815 and was sent to a series of frontier posts.

In 1831 Bonneville took a two-year leave from the Army, ostensibly to try his hand in the fur trade. He did so poorly in the fur business, though, while exploring extensively, that historians suspect he may have been secretly by the government to collect information beyond its frontiers. South Pass was more or less where the United States, Mexico and British Oregon met.

What is known of Bonneville's travels comes mainly from Washington Irving's biography, *The Adventures of Captain Bonneville,* compiled from a manuscript the Captain wrote after his return. The result is an account that has frustrated scholars with its frequent inaccuracy, while giving a vivid picture of the West in the 1830s.

Bonneville left Missouri in May 1832, leading a company of 100 trappers, hunters, swampers and packers. He was also performing an experiment that turned out to be of historical significance: he hauled 20 wagons over the Continental Divide.

Crossing South Pass with what remained of the wagons, Bonneville built a post under the west flank of the Wind Rivers where Horse Creek joins the Green, near present-day Daniel Junction and the convergence of U.S. 189 and 191; skeptical mountain men christened it "Fort Nonsense." In August, learning that the upper Green was a cold, windy place in winter, he left the wagons and headed up the Green, crossing the north end of the Wind Rivers, apparently by Union Pass, then continuing to Jackson Hole, presumably via Togwotee Pass. After wintering in Idaho, Bonneville returned to the Green River in time for the 1833 Rendezvous, which took place near his fort.

In late July, Bonneville cached supplies and led his men across South Pass, intending to trap along tributaries of the Bighorn. The trappers, though, were harassed by Blackfeet, who so depleted them of traps that Bonneville decided to return with three or four men (Irving's count varies) to his Green River cache to resupply. Not wanting to repeat the circuitous route through South Pass, he tried a direct route across the Wind Rivers.

"The mountains were lofty, with snowy peaks and cragged sides," according to Washington Irving. "It was hoped, however, that some practicable defile might be found." Bonneville and his companions first tried one of the branches of the Popo Agie but were turned back; all branches of this river issue from the mountains through rough gorges that even today are not

Capt. Benjamin Bonneville was given leave by the Army to engage in the fur trade, but he was far more successful as an explorer than as a businessman. WYOMING STATE ARCHIVES, MUSEUMS AND HISTORICAL DEPARTMENT

amenable to trails. They recalled, however, having seen a slope that appeared to rise continuously to "the snowy region"; the lower slopes of the east side of the range do indeed gradually rise and appear from the Wind River Valley to reach a plateau just below the crest.

Instead of the hoped-for plateau, however, Bonneville found "the brink of a deep and precipitous ravine, from the bottom of which rose a second slope, similar to the one...just ascended." He descended into this ravine and ascended the second slope, only to find another ravine and another slope. They realized that what had seemed a continuous slope "was shagged by frightful precipices, and seamed with longitudinal chasms, deep and dangerous."

Nevertheless, the trappers continued and two days later found themselves in "the heart of this mountainous and awful solitude." Or so Irving described their situation, even if he also placed them that evening at "two bright and beautiful little lakes, set like mirrors in the midst of stern and rocky heights, and surrounded by grassy meadows, inexpressibly refreshing to the eye."

Leaving two men with the horses, the Captain and one or two companions set out among the "huge crags of granite piled one upon another, and beetling like battlements far above them," hoping to discover a route through the range. Choosing from the "gigantic peaks...towering far into the snowy regions of the atmosphere" the summit that appeared highest, these first white men known to have penetrated the Wind Rivers began to climb. The climbing was difficult enough that the men were "frequently obliged to clamber on hands and knees, with their guns slung upon their backs" and "frequently, exhausted with fatigue...threw themselves upon the snow, and took handfuls of it to allay their parching thirst." But, according to Bonneville's biographer, "the pride of man is never more obstinate than when climbing mountains."

At this point in Irving's narrative, there occurs one of the most anticlimactic sentences in the annals of western exploration, one that has confounded those who have tried to identify Bonneville's peak. "At one place," wrote Irving, "they even stripped off their coats and hung them upon the bushes." This and cooling breezes seemed to reinvigorate the men, for "springing with new ardor to their task," they soon stood on the summit.

"Here a scene burst upon the view of Captain Bonneville, that for a time astonished and overwhelmed him with its immensity. He stood, in fact, upon that dividing ridge which Indians regard as the crest of the world"— and which whites regard as the Continental Divide.

"Whichever way he turned his eye, it was confounded by the vastness and variety of objects. Beneath him, the Rocky Mountains seemed to open all their secret recesses; deep solemn valleys; treasured lakes; dreary passes; rugged defiles and foaming torrents; while beyond their savage precincts, the eye was lost in an almost immeasurable landscape….Whichever way he looked, he beheld vast plains glimmering with reflected sunshine; mighty streams wandering on their shining course toward either ocean, and snowy mountains, chain beyond chain, and peak beyond peak, till they melted like clouds into the horizon."

Irving gives a "simple enumeration of….features…of this vast panorama" in order to "give some idea of its collective grandeur." It is this enumeration that has most confused efforts to identify the peak. The catalogue of sights includes the Sweetwater, "pursuing its tranquil way through the rugged regions of the Black Hills"; the Wind River to the east, which "forced [its] way through the range of Horn Mountains"; to the north, "glimpses of the upper streams of the Yellowstone"; "some of the sources of the…Columbia, flowing…past those towering landmarks, the Three Tetons, and pouring down into the great lava plain"; and "almost at the captain's feet, the Green River…dashing northward over crag and precipice…and tumbling into the plain, where, expanding into an ample river, it circled away to the south."

The Tetons can be seen from many northern Wind River summits and a few southern summits. The proximity of the Green to the captain's feet, his opinion that he stood on "the loftiest point of the North American continent" (he estimated its elevation at 25,000') and, more significantly, his knowing the trick of the river's bend from north to south, has been cited as evidence that he must have climbed Gannett Peak. However, even ignoring the bushes, which must be ignored when supporting any hypothesis, the Sweetwater cannot be seen from Gannett, nor would Gannett be reached from the Popo Agie. Bonneville crossed Union Pass both the year before his climb and just after it, and would have passed the Big Bend. And, despite Irving's assurance that "the atmosphere [was] so pure that objects were discernible at an astonishing distance," no tributaries of the Yellowstone are visible from the Wind Rivers, nor are the lava plains where the Snake crosses Idaho.

An odd-sounding theory was propounded in 1924 that Bonneville's peak was Mt. Chauvenet, which we know as an obscure 12,250' peak unmistakably east of the Divide and within sight of obviously higher peaks. The theory becomes intriguing only after close scrutiny of the map produced by the Hayden Survey of 1877-1878. The name of Survey topographer Louis Chauvenet is attached to the peak we know as Lizard Head, at 12,842' the highest summit in the Cirque of the Towers, the third highest in the southern Wind Rivers. Did explorers of the 1830s find their way to the well-hidden, relatively inaccessible Cirque? The geography of their approach march makes the possibility unlikely, though one would like to imagine Bonneville contemplating the array of Warbonnet, Shark's Nose, Overhanging Tower and Pingora standing between him and his destination.

Also on the Hayden Survey map, the name Mt. Bonneville sits where the name Raid Peak sits today. Why Bonneville's name became associated with Raid Peak, unless simply to honor the early explorer, is incomprehensible. Raid Peak is not only west of the Divide; its 1,800' east face is one of the highest, steepest walls in the range, while its west slopes lead gently to meadows and forests that descend to the Green River Valley. By the time of the 1938 topographic map, however, the name Mt. Bonneville had moved' to the most inaccessible peak of the region, which repulsed all attempts to climb it until 1946.

Trying to pin down the identity of Bonneville's summit is futile, and it also misses the point. The Captain stood on some Wind River summit; he saw, in general terms, what can be seen from many Wind Rivers summits, and he seems to have appreciated the scenery as deeply as a modern recreational climber. Nor should Irving be faulted for accuracy. He conveyed the flavor of a Wind River view remarkably well for an Easterner who never was there.

However inspired by the view from his summit, Bonneville saw that crossing the Wind River crest on horse was impracticable. After an adventurous retreat, the Captain and his men circled through South Pass, resupplied at the Fort Nonsense cache, and crossed Union Pass to the head of the Wind River, where he had arranged to meet the main body of his trappers.

Bonneville's further adventures in the West—his claim to have discovered Great Salt Lake's lack of outlet and attempt to name the lake for himself; the discovery by his lieutenant, Joseph Walker, of Yosemite Valley—belong to the history of other parts of the West.

Bonneville finally returned East in 1835, two years after his leave expired. The Army had written him off as "virtually dead or lost." It was while politicking to be reinstated that he met Irving. His pardon and reinstatement by a noted disciplinarian, President Andrew Jackson, has fueled the speculation that Bonneville was being rewarded for reconnaissance of foreign territory, through which Oregon or California might be invaded. Bonneville fought in the Mexican War, served as a recruiting officer during the Civil War, and retired, in 1866, a brigadier general.

Miller's *"Indian Encampment near the Wind River Mountains."* Several tribes attended the annual fur rendezvous, for business and for pleasure. The gentleman smoking the ceremonial pipe probably is Miller's employer, Sir William Drummond Stewart. BUFFALO BILL HISTORICAL CENTER

Louis-Joseph's vague account is almost the only source of information about the Verendryes' journey. The identity of the various Indian tribes has been a subject of conjecture and debate. The mountains seen beyond the Snake People village have been identified as the Black Hills, the Big-horns, the Wind Rivers and ranges farther west. Twentieth-century historians, however, have been more cautious in placing the Verendryes beyond the Black Hills or Big-horns, since in 1913 a girl in Pierre, South Dakota found the lead plate sticking out of the ground.

When Lewis and Clark descended the Missouri in 1806, returning from their epic crossing of the continent, they met two trappers ascending. The trappers wanted someone who had been upriver as a guide, and John Colter turned his back on civilization, which he had not seen in two years and joined them. Colter descended the Missouri again the next year and again met trappers who persuaded him to return to the mountains.

From the junction of the Missouri and Bighorn, Colter went south and west on a solitary journey that is among the persistent legends of northwest Wyoming—all the more legendary because the only record of the journey that survives is a map Clark drew after Colter visited him in St. Louis in 1814. For several decades Colter's credibility was low, because of his reports of "hidden fires, smoking pits, noxious streams, and the all-pervading smell of brimstone" near the headwaters of the Yellowstone. Jokes about "Colter's Hell" for a time obscured the fact that he probably—according to a modern consensus—ascended the Wind River, crossed Union Pass, and descended the Gros Ventre to Jackson Hole.

Colter may have been the first white to see the Wind Rivers, but such distinctions are always uncertain, for most documented explorers were preceded by unrecorded trappers and wanderers. In 1811 John Jacob Astor sent a party, led by Wilson Price Hunt, to establish a fur post at the mouth of the Columbia—an expedition that made the next recorded crossing of the continent after Lewis and Clark. On the Missouri River they met three trappers—John Hoback, Jacob Rizner and Edward Robinson—returning east after several years in the mountains. Like Colter, they had apparently become homesick for the high country: they went back as Hunt's guides.

wandered around the Dakotas, spending weeks visiting other Indians. The Horse People were afraid to venture farther west because of fearsome Snake People, so the Verendryes joined the Bow People, who were planning war against the Snake People. The Bow People reported that the Snake People lived at the base of high mountains and had heard from Snake prisoners that from these mountains could be seen a sea on which White men lived. When mountains came in sight to the west, the war party found a deserted Snake People village, which they interpreted to mean that the Snake People had circled them and were massacring Bow People women and children. This was the closest the Verendryes came to the Western Sea. On the way back Louis-Joseph buried a lead plate claiming the West for France.

Hunt had planned to follow the route of Lewis and Clark up the Missouri, but his three guides convinced him that the danger of an encounter with hostile Blackfeet was too great on the Missouri and that they knew an easier way through the mountains. They led the Astorians around the Bighorns, followed the Wind River to its head, crossed Union Pass to the Green and then crossed the Rim—the Divide between the Green and the Snake—to the tributary of the Snake now named for Hoback, and so continued to Oregon. The question lingers: How much of the West had Hoback, Riznor and Robinson seen before meeting the Astorians? They apparently had not seen the pass that was to prove far more important than Union Pass.

South Pass did not enter our history with a flourish. In June 1812, Robert Stuart, a Scot immigrant who had sailed to Astoria from New York, led an overland party east with the first dispatches Astor would receive from his Pacific post. Near the Snake River in eastern Idaho, Crow Indians ran off Stuart's horses, and the the Astorians wandered on foot, destitute, west of the Tetons, then across Teton Pass to Jackson Hole. Shoshones told them of South Pass, and Stuart led his men across the Rim into the Green River Valley. They had been without food for a week, when a French-Canadian proposed the grim casting of lots that seems obligatory to the scenario of starving men. Stuart cocked his rifle and vetoed the proposal; the next day they found and killed a solitary decrepit buffalo.

Stuart's party continued southeast along the west edge of the "Spanish River Mountains"—the Wind Rivers—meeting Shoshones who had lost all but one horse to the Crows; this old horse they traded to the Astorians. With a supply of meat strapped to their pack animal, the men continued. The Astorians' route from the Green River Valley is more a matter of historical tradition than a line that can be traced on a map, for while Stuart's account is full of details, including distances and directions for each day's travel, the sagebrush plains between the Green River and South Pass are nondescript, and Stuart's springs and ridges cannot be identified with actual features. Having been warned by the Shoshones of Crows camped in the pass, the white men skirted somewhat south of the pass proper—a detail of interest only to those who worry about the first true white crossing of South Pass. The Astorians descended the Sweetwater to the North Platte, and so reached civilization.

(continued on page 74)

The Ascent of Frémont Peak

In 1842 an obscure young lieutenant of topographical engineers, known only for eloping with the daughter of the most powerful man in the U.S. Senate, took a steamboat up the Missouri from St. Louis. Also on the steamer was a practitioner of one of the most obscure professions, Rocky Mountain fur trapper. That was how John C. Frémont met Kit Carson. The Army was sending Frémont west to survey the wagon road, not yet called the Oregon Trail, as far as South Pass and to suggest sites for military posts. Carson had tried returning to civilization after 16 years in the West; he says in his autobiography that he stayed in St. Louis "a few days," became "tired of the settlements," and decided he preferred mountain life.

The two hit it off; Carson told Frémont "that I had been some time in the mountains and thought I could guide him to any point he would wish to go. He replied that he would make inquiry regarding my qualifications." Apparently the references were favorable; Frémont—who later ran for president as "The Pathfinder"—hired Carson as scout, adding him to a party that already included many experienced trappers.

Frémont and Carson could hardly have had less similar backgrounds. Frémont's father had fled France when his side lost the Revolution. En route to Santo Domingo, his ship was captured by a British man-of-war. Offered a choice between prison and America, Fremont *pere* (his son, the explorer, added the accent to the family name) became a French teacher in Virginia. Here he ran off to Savannah with an elderly planter's young wife, who became the mother of the surveyor. The Virginia marriage was never properly dissolved, so when Frémont stood before Thomas Hart Benton to announce that he had married Jessie, the Senator's daughter, his list of stigmas included illegitimacy. Benson, however, was above all else an advocate of western expansion and saw in his bold, energetic son-in-law an agent for his policies. He arranged for Frémont to be sent west.

Carson was orphaned at a young age in Missouri. An ad that appeared in an 1826 *Missouri Intelligencer* summarizes his youth and the start of his career in the West:

"Notice is hereby given to all persons, That Christopher Carson, a boy about 16 years old, small of his age, but thick-set; light hair, ran away from the subscriber, living in Franklin, Howard County, Missouri, to whom he had been bound to learn the saddler's trade, on or about the first of September last. He is supposed to have made his way to the upper part of the state. All persons are notified not to harbor, support, or assist said boy under the penalty of the law. One cent reward will be given to any person who will bring back the said boy."

Jessie Frémont had a literary talent that could polish a technical report into a heroic saga. But one element she did not work into Frémont's *Report of the Exploring Expedition to the Rocky Mountains in the year 1842* that would have accentuated his role as romantic adventurer: a foil, a cynical Sancho Panza lacking the hero's vision. Charles Preuss compensated for this defect in his *Exploring with Frémont*. Preuss was an unemployed German immigrant with an impoverished family when Frémont hired him as cartographer and artist. However, Preuss never let gratitude stand between him and his disdain for the West and the man who dragged him through it.

Exploring with Frémont is Preuss's diary, never polished for publication. Some days' entries are pointedly terse, especially when crossing the prairies: "Murky weather, melancholy mood"; "Nothing but prairie. Made twenty miles. Very hot." On other days he discourses more freely about the food or the mosquitos: "For breakfast, yesterday's dish was warmed up; it did not taste excellent"; "Had a remarkably bad night.... The others lay safely under their [mosquito] nets; mine had been forgotten because of Frémont's negligence." Frémont provoked Preuss's longest commentaries. Here is Preuss on Frémont, when Carson got too far ahead of the party:

"This and other small troubles and annoyances had gotten on Frémont's nerves, which is not all surprising with a childishly passionate man like him. In consequence he decided to let this be the end of the expedition and go straightway back to the Sweet Water.... He imparted the news to me last night, and who was happier than I? I gladly agreed to all his reasons, whether good or bad."

Preuss senses "a certain tension, not only between Frémont and myself, but also between me and the rest of the people. Only, of course, because I want to be smarter than the others." A temperamental leader and the scruffy voyageurs Frémont recruited in St. Louis could not have been ideal companions for a sensitive topographer.

Here is Preuss approaching the Wind Rivers:

"Whoever has seen Switzerland and expects something similar here is bound for a great disappointment. An American has measured them to be as high as 25,000 feet. I'll be hanged if they are half as high, yea, if they are 8,000 feet high. A little snow on their peaks; that is all, as far as I can see now, that distinguishes them from other high mountains.

"I am reminded of the day when I walked from Liestal to Solethurn. When I came around a corner of rocks, I saw in front of me the entire range of the Alps from Mont Blanc to the Alps of Tirol. If I compare that view with the

Above: *This small peak, known as Elephant Head, rises east of Island Lake.*
Facing page: *The veteran mountain men who guided John C. Frémont were of the opinion that this peak, seen here from Island Lake, was the highest in the Rockies.*
PAT O'HARA PHOTOS

one I see today, it is as though I were to turn my eyes from the face of a lovely girl to the wrinkled face of an old woman."

It must be added that Preuss never let his feelings for Frémont and the West prevent him from going west with Frémont; he was on Frémont's expedition the next year to Oregon and California and on the disastrous attempt in the winter of 1848-1849 to cross the Sangre de Cristos, in Colorado. It must further added that Preuss was a brave man who handled himself well in emergencies and that he produced the first competent maps of the West, resisting the temptation to incorporate the hearsay that plagued most early maps.

Frémont's assignment was to explore as far as South Pass. But his mountain veterans expressed the opinion that the Wind Rivers included the highest peak in the Rockies. It would be interesting to know their reasoning, without transit or barometer, but all that survives is one sentence in Frémont's *Report:*

"From the description given by Mackenzie of the mountains where he crossed them [in Canada], with that of a French officer still farther to the north, and Colonel Long's measurements to the south, joined to the opinion of the oldest traders of the country, it is presumed that this is the highest peak of the Rocky mountains."

According to Frémont, the height of this peak "had been a theme of constant discussion." There was, therefore, general enthusiasm for getting the valued barometer to the top.

Frémont led his entourage along the west flank of the range, camping one night on the East Fork River, the next night by Boulder Lake. With 15 men mounted on mules, Frémont then headed toward the high peaks. The country they passed through is a complicated topography of small hills, crooked streams and many lakes; even the guides were surprised by one group of lakes. That day's route cannot be traced, but evening found them in one of those classic little fault-line valleys—"smoothly carpeted with a soft grass, and scattered over with groups of flowers"— this one occupied by Monument Creek.

While the modern topographic map does not indicate a trail paralleling Monument Creek, nor is one maintained, a well-beaten way leads to the pass at its head. Here the high peaks of Titcomb Basin suddenly come into view: "a gigantic disorder of enormous masses, and a savage sublimity of naked rock, in wonderful contrast with innumerable green spots of a rich floral beauty, shut up in their stern recesses."

The going beyond was obviously rocky, so three men stayed to guard the mules while the others proceeded on foot. Frémont Peak looks deceptively close from the pass above Monument Creek. It appeared so close to Frémont and his men that, expecting to climb it and return that day, they took little clothing and no food—except Preuss: "only I, a more experienced mountaineer, stuck a piece of dried buffalo meat in my pocket."

They descended to Little Seneca Lake, where the Highline now crosses the Island Lake Trail. The next few miles are frustrating going for a modern backpacker, who at the end of a 12-mile day may find slight consolation in recognizing the route in Frémont's century-old description:

"The first ridge hid a succession of others; and when, with great fatigue and difficulty, we had climbed up five hundred feet, it was but to make an equal descent on the other side.... We clambered on, always expecting, with every ridge that we crossed, to reach the foot of the peaks, and always disappointed, until...pretty well worn out, we reached the shore of a little lake, in which there was a rocky island."

Thus the name Island Lake, which was the only place name Frémont left in the Wind Rivers and one of the surprisingly few anywhere in the West (Golden Gate, however, was one of the others). The men made what camp their scant provisions allowed on a bluff overlooking Island Lake, near falls that drop to the lake from Titcomb Basin.

Before Island Lake, according to Preuss, "The leader, Carson walked too fast. This caused some exchange of words. Frémont got excited, as usual, and designated a young chap to take the lead—he could not serve as a guide, of course. Frémont developed a headache...." In fact, although the effects of altitude were not well known in those premountaineering days, Frémont's commentary, as well as Preuss's, gives ample evidence that the leader suffered altitude sickness more than most.

The wind and cold of the dinnerless, blanketless bivouac did not improve Frémont's condition, and as for Preuss, "as always, the best spots were already taken...and I can truthfully say that I did not sleep a single minute"; both mention being glad when dawn eventually lightened the sky. That day, August 14, was not one of successful expeditionary mountaineering. The party evidently approached their objective via Indian Basin, but became badly scattered, each trying to find a feasible route. Frémont became progressively sicker and eventually was unable to go farther. Two of the French-Canadians also became ill and lay down on rocks. Preuss, trying to make his way across a snow field, slipped and fell a few hundred feet into the rocks, where "he turned a couple of somersets" but survived with only minor bruises. Nevertheless, amid the chaos, Carson climbed the Divide peak to the right of their objective, to see if he could cross to the main peak. He could not, and he did not deem this ascent worth mention in his autobiography, but Carson evidently climbed 13,517′ Jackson Peak—the second reported ascent in the Wind Rivers, the first of an identifiable peak and the first 13,000-footer (unless Bonneville climbed Wind River Peak).

Meanwhile, men went back for mules, blankets and food, and the second night at Island Lake was more comfortable than the first. Frémont, expecting to start back to the low country in the morning, had instructed Carson to set out ahead of him at dawn, which Carson did. However, the remaining men—Frémont, Preuss, Basil Lajeunesse, Clement Lambert, Johnny Janisse and de Coteau or Descoteaux—felt well enough for another try, mounted mules, and headed up "a defile of the most rugged mountains known." This defile was probably Titcomb Basin, though it could have been Indian Basin; in either they would have found themselves "riding along the huge wall which forms the central summits of the chain…terminating 2,000 to 3,000 feet above…in a serrated line of broken, jagged cones" and encountered "three small lakes of a green color, each of perhaps a thousand yards in diameter."

Leaving the mules to graze, the six climbers set out on foot, making a point to take their time and rest when tired. Halfway up, Frémont changed from thick-soled moccasins to a thinner pair, "as now the use of our toes became necessary to a further advance." The route taken by Frémont is today rated class 3, meaning that hand holds must be used, though the difficulty is not great enough (at least for climbers in rubber-soled boots) to warrant a rope. Nevertheless, some route-finding is required, and Frémont describes circling an overhang and surmounting a crack by jamming hands and feet. Upon reaching the crest, Frémont "sprang upon the summit, and another step would have precipitated me into an immense snow field five hundred feet below"—the square-mile Upper Frémont Glacier.

The victorious climbers rammed a pole into a crevice, attached the American flag to it and admired the setting:

"Around us, the whole scene had one main striking feature, which was that of terrible convulsion. Parallel to its length, the ridge was split into chasms and fissures; between which rose the thin lofty walls, terminated with slender minarets and columns."

Today, a climber atop Frémont Peak sees tents at Island Lake and in Titcomb Basin and perhaps hears the shout "Off belay!" reverberate off the walls. Frémont reminds us how isolated he and his men were, how empty the Wind Rivers were in terms of humanity:

"A stillness the most profound and a terrible solitude forced themselves constantly on the mind as the great features of the place. Here, on the summit…the stillness was absolute, unbroken by any sound, and the solitude complete."

In the vast landscape Frémont could see from his summit were only Carson and his companions, perhaps a few Sheepeater Indians, perhaps a few Plains Indians in the Green River Valley.

Frémont used his barometer to ascertain an elevation of 13,570′ above sea level—remarkably close to the 13,745′ on current topographic maps. Preuss in his diary, no doubt to spite Frémont, guesses that the barometer readings "will probably correspond to almost 10,000 feet."

Preuss did not keep his diary for several days, and had much catching up to do after the climb. His entries then give the impression that he was as anxious as the others to reach the top and was pleased with the climb. His one complaint is that Frémont did not give him enough time on top to make measurements and that "when the time comes for me to make my map in Washington, he will more than regret this unwise haste."

One senses Jessie's hand behind her husband's reflection as he left the summit:

"We had accomplished an object of laudable ambition, and beyond the strict order of our instructions. We had climbed the loftiest peak of the Rocky mountains, and looked down upon the snow a thousand feet below, and, standing where never human foot had stood before, felt the exultation of first explorers."

Above: *Sunset at Brooks Lake, near Togwotee Pass.*
Right: *Little is known about the inhabitants of the area before Shoshones and Crows arrived within the past several centuries. The most vivid evidences of their presence left by the ancients are petroglyphs pecked in east-side canyon walls.*
BILL LANCASTER PHOTOS

Jedediah Smith

Whether the returning Astorians discovered South Pass is a question of semantics; it did not stay discovered. The honor of being "effective discoverers" (Dale Morgan and Bernard DeVoto both used the phrase) belongs to a group led by Jedediah Smith, who was after Lewis and Clark our greatest western explorer.

In February, 1822, William Ashley placed an ad in the *Missouri Gazette* that began: "To Enterprising Young Men: The subscriber wishes to engage One Hundred Men, to ascend the river Missouri to its source, there to be em-

More important than precisely where they crossed the Divide was that the Astorians, more intent on avoiding the Crows than in pathfinding, did not appreciate the significance of their discovery. The post of Astoria soon was abandoned, because of the War of 1812, and South Pass—to the extent anyone knew of it—was forgotten.

ployed for one, two or three years. For particulars...." Jim Clyman, one of the few literate men attracted by the ad, later wrote: "A discription of our crew I cannt give but Falstafs Battalion was genteel in comparison." But it, and a similar ad the next year, brought to the mountains Smith, Clyman, Jim Bridger, Thomas Fitzpatick, David Jackson, William Sublette and others destined to leave a mark on western history.

Previous fur entrepreneurs had established posts to which Indians brought furs to trade. Ashley's scheme was to have his men do the actual trapping. And while their predecessors went up the Missouri by keelboat, Ashley's men traveled overland, on horse. Thus was born the mountain man, setting traps in icy streams, riding with his loaded Hawken rifle across his lap, his wary eyes scanning a distant horizon for signs of game and of Indians.

Trapping required more exploration than trading did, and Smith in particular was always on the lookout for new streams. During the winter of 1823-1824 he and a party that included Fitzpatrick, Clyman and Sublette reached the Crows on the Wind River. The Crows reported especially plentiful beaver on the other side of the Wind Rivers. In February 1824, the trappers ascended the Wind River Valley and tried to cross Union Pass but were turned back by snow.

They returned to the Crows, where, according to Clyman, "I spread out a buffalo Robe and covered it with sand, and made it in heaps to represent the different mountains.... From our sand map with the help of the Crows, [we] finally got the idea that we could go to Green River, called by them Seeds-ka-day."

This primitive map sent Clyman and his companions up the Popo Agie, around the south end of the Wind Rivers and through South Pass. However, Clyman and Sublette nearly froze while hunting, and when the party reached the Sweetwater, the wind was so strong that the men were awake all night keeping their blankets from blowing away. In the morning the wind was still too strong for a fire. They waited behind a clump of willows all that day and the next night, but the wind did not let up. The following morning they shot a "mountain sheep" (which might be either a bighorn sheep or a pronghorn antelope) but again could not start a fire to cook it. Finally, the second night, the wind died down enough for Clyman to light a fire, and the men spent the rest of the night broiling slices of meat. The next day—during a heavy snow—they moved camp down to an aspen grove in a valley, and there they stayed for several weeks.

When game ran out in mid-March, Smith and his men were forced to resume their journey. But they were confronted with a continuing ground blizzard, and on the sixth day they were in a desperate situation, having not eaten for four days, when Sublette and Clyman shot a buffalo. They were again unable to light a fire but were by then beyond requiring that the meat be cooked. Their next need was water that was not frozen, but they continued all that day without coming to a stream. Thus was South Pass crossed by Americans from east to west for the first time and permanently discovered, even if Smith was unaware of the crossing until he noted the slope of the land the next day, when he still was more concerned with water and warmth than geography.

Summer's end is signaled by heavy snow. An Indian summer that follows can be an especially good time to be in the mountains, although a traveler must be prepared for further storms.
BARBARA & MICHAEL PFLAUM

South Pass is not a dramatic alpine gap, a notch in a jagged spine that obviously separates two torrents. John Frémont, the first surveyor by, had trouble locating the height of land in the 12 miles between Atlantic water and Pacific water: "We were obliged to watch very closely to find the place at which we had reached the culminating point." He estimated the rise as being comparable "to the ascent of the Capitol hill" and mused on the use of the word "pass" in a place that "in no manner resembles the places to which the term is commonly applied—nothing of the gorge-like character and winding ascents of the Allegheny passes in America: nothing of the Great St. Bernard and Simplon passes in Europe." A modern traveler, despite a highway turnoff and marker, may be equally skeptical. But this lack of topographic drama is responsible for South Pass's dramatic role in American history.

When Smith and his fellow explorers reached the Little Sandy, according to Clyman, the thirsty men "went immediately to cutting the ice with their Tomahauks caled out frose to the bottom." But Clyman shot a pistol into a hole, and water came spurting up. Less eventfully, Smith's party reached the Green. Within a few years the Green River Valley was the heartland of the thriving Rocky Mountain fur business.

(continued on page 80)

Haystack Mountain dominates the valley of Clear and Deep lakes.
DENNIS J. CWIDAK

William Drummond Stewart

In spring 1833, the Scotsman William Drummond Stewart arrived in St. Louis, wanting to see the West. He had served as a captain under Wellington at Waterloo, but an older brother inherited the family barony of Grandtully. The captain was between jobs, the Rocky Mountains' first recreational visitor. In St. Louis he fell in with the firm of Sublette and Campbell, who outfitted the Rocky Mountain Fur Company's Rendezvous. Stewart traveled with Robert Campbell to Rendezvous, held that year where Horse Creek meets the Green, near Bonneville's Fort Nonsense. Stewart's military training made him a useful member of a pack train, especially in country where Indians might run off unguarded horses. He enforced military discipline on a party, took his turn standing night guard, and during his years in the West fought in dozens of Indian skirmishes. He won the respect of a tough bunch. Kit Carson wrote in his autobiography that Stewart "will be forever remembered for his liberality and his many good qualities by the mountaineers who had the honor of his acquaintance."

Stewart accompanied Tom Fitzpatrick on his fall trapping excursion through northern Wyoming and southern Montana—Crow country—then apparently wintered in the West, perhaps with Jim Bridger's brigade on the Green River. The summer of 1834 found Stewart again at Rendezvous, this one on Ham's Fork in southwestern Wyoming. Stewart returned to the West and Rendezvous each summer until 1839.

Stewart brought fast horses from St. Louis and often won the wild races trappers and Indians staged at Rendezvous. Mountain men were notorious for their liaisons with native women. Stewart did have a wife back in Scotland, but one gathers there was not much passion—he sailed for America two years after marrying and did not return for seven years—and there are indications that the handsome captain took part in the amorous side of mountain man life and indeed was a favorite of the Indian women.

Beaver fur was most valuable when taken in spring or fall; summer was a trapper's time to relax. After a Rendezvous, Stewart would invite his friends to one of the large lakes on the Wind Rivers' west slope (Frémont and New Fork are two for which we have evidence) for a week or two of fishing, hunting and enjoying the captain's fine ports and brandies.

These were portentous times to be in the Wyoming mountains. Important travelers setting out for, or returning from, the West paid a call on St. Louis's most distinguished citizen, William Clark. Jim Bridger and Kit Carson were fur brigade leaders. In 1833 the Scottish captain met the American Captain Bonneville. After the 1834 Rendezvous, Stewart traveled to Oregon with a party that included pioneer botanists/ornithologists Thomas Nuttall and John Kirk Townsend and the first emigrant to follow what became the

Oregon Trail, Jason Lee. Lee went West as a missionary, but as the first white settler in the Willamette Valley he encouraged the migration of the next decade. In 1836 the supply train, with which Stewart traveled west, included Narcissa Whitman and Eliza Spalding—missionaries' wives headed to Oregon and the first white women across South Pass.

Traveling west with Indians to the 1838 Rendezvous was an unlikely Swiss who had left home to escape debtors' prison. While obsessed with a desire to reach the Pacific Coast, he knew little about the country or why he

In this view of the 1837 Rendezvous, on the Green River, Frémont Peak can be seen on the right skyline. The watercolor was painted by famed pioneer photographer William H. Jackson. Although he was born in 1843, three years after the last rendezvous on the Green River, Jackson reconstructed such scenes from descriptions by Irving, Fremont, and innumerable newspapers of the day.
DENVER PUBLIC LIBRARY, WESTERN HISTORY DEPARTMENT

wanted to be there. This was Johann Augustus Sutter, whose presence in the mountains was as portentous as those of more purposeful travelers. He continued to California and gold rush fame, and his story belongs not to the Wind Rivers but to the Sierra Nevada.

In 1837, Stewart, perhaps sensing that a way of life was ending, or that his days in the West were limited, decided to capture the scene, create a sort of time capsule. In New Orleans he found the studio of a young painter named Alfred Jacob Miller. He admired a view of Baltimore that Miller was completing and hired him to go West. On the Sweetwater the young artist was absorbed in a painting when his head was suddenly grabbed from behind and forced down. It was the captain teaching him to be more alert for Indians.

Rendezvous that year was again on the Green, between Horse Creek and the New Fork. Stewart surprised his friend Bridger with an improbable gift—a suit of medieval armor, which must have been sent from Scotland. Toward the end of Rendezvous, Stewart took Miller and some of the mountain men up to the lake that was once called Stewart's Lake but which we now call Frémont Lake; it can be identified from a Miller painting. Miller's notes mention casks of brandy and of port. They also mention trout that "were unsophisticated and bit immediately we placed the bait near their mouths in the clear water." While most of the party fished and hunted, Miller busily sketched the scenery—the earliest surviving illustrations of the Wind Rivers.

Stewart and Miller then joined a fall trapping expedition that passed by the Tetons and through the Wind River Valley, before the sportsman and the artist returned to St. Louis.

Stewart's brother died in 1838, and in 1839 he returned to Scotland, Sir William, Baronet of Grandtully. He did not, however, completely leave the Wind Rivers behind. He brought his mixed-blood hunting guide, Antoine Clement, as a sort of valet/gamekeeper. He wrote William Sublette, asking him to send buffalo. The grounds of Stewart's estate included Birnam Wood, and the spectacle of a home where buffalo roamed must have seemed as strange to the Scots as the encroachment of the forest did to Macbeth. Miller came to finish converting his watercolor sketches to oils, which took their place with a Caravaggio, a Correggio, a Raphael and a da Vinci.

Stewart returned to the American West in 1843, but the golden age had passed. The last Rendezvous had been held in 1838, and Stewart's expedition set out with newspaper publicity and rich dudes paying their way. He did not return to America again.

Bernard DeVoto wrote that Stewart's wanderlust put him in a class of men to whom campaigning and battle had been a climactic experience, giving them a sense of reality and function surpassing anything peace had to offer, convincing them that in extremity they had been most truly themselves, and leaving them to spend the rest of their lives looking for an experience, any kind of experience, that…would restore the lost splendor. Stewart came closest to finding it in the Far West.

Stewart wrote two murky novels set in the west he saw—*Edward Warren* and *Altowan*. DeVoto described these novels as "wooden and absurd," adding that they "dwell repeatedly on mysterious longings and melancholies, romantic passions, unhappiness and frustration, an urgent but never quite focused unrest." Much of the melancholies and passions take place on the New Fork River and by headwater lakes in the northern Wind Rivers, where exiled heroes and mysterious women with "lustrous, raven locks" undergo various permutations of pursuit and capture by kleptomaniac Crows (Stewart's revenge for their theft of his horses) and noble Blackfeet led by a white chief.

It was not Stewart's novels that are responsible for his small measure of 20th-century fame, but the hundred watercolors Miller painted in 1837. A Mrs. Clyde Porter saw Miller's paintings in a Philadelphia museum and, recognizing them as depictions of the fur trade, purchased them. Wanting to publish what she had discovered, Mrs. Porter looked for a historian to provide captions and an introductory essay. DeVoto, realizing that Miller's were the only existing pictures of many aspects of a fascinating time, accepted the assignment and set aside a month for the project. But as he delved into the story behind the paintings, DeVoto became aware that Stewart had seen so many important Rocky Mountain events during the 1830s that he could use Stewart "as a line to hang the whole fur trade on." The result, two years later, was a book, *Across the Wide Missouri,* which comes close to being a history of the fur trade, especially in the Wind River area during the 1830s. Accused by historians of reading too much like a novel, *Across the Wide Missouri* manages to emphasize the romanticism of life in a scenic wilderness lived by men highly skilled in a difficult, dangerous profession. Stewart eventually progressed from art to art history to American history to novel to the silver screen. When Hollywood made a movie of *Across the Wide Missouri,* Clark Gable played Stewart. A look at one of Miller's sketches in which a tall, dark, mustached, aquiline-nosed figure—obviously the artist's employer—sits on a white horse as the central figure in a tableau, surrounded by admiring Indians, suggests why Gable was chosen for the role.

"Greeting the Trappers," one of Alfred Jacob Miller's depictions of the 1837
Rendezvous, held on the Green River. BUFFALO BILL HISTORICAL CENTER

Sunsets on Mts. Helen (left) and Sacagawea (right), which form the east wall of upper Titcomb Basin.
CHARLIE CRANGLE

upon the previous summer. The pack train returned east in August with a year's fur harvest. The first Rendezvous was held in 1825, on the Green River. Seven subsequent Rendezvous were held in the Green River Valley, two on the Popo Agie and several at sites farther from the Wind Rivers.

A Rendezvous, which lasted three weeks, was more than an exchange of fur for supplies; it was the social event of the Rocky Mountains. Trapping was a solitary profession, and trappers—independents as well as company men—came not only to trade but also to renew friendships, hear the news from the States and enjoy themselves. Shoshones, Flatheads and Nez Perces also came to trade and celebrate, scattering hundreds of tipis over the prairie, adding to the pageantry by dancing, chanting, showing off their horses and staging mock battles.

If a teetotaler could be found, he was engaged to dispense the whiskey, which had been diluted with Green River water (the same principle as freeze-dried food). As the trappers became drunker, the alcohol was further diluted. A drunken trapper was in no mood to quibble about prices, and he soon spent his year's furs on whiskey, the next year's supplies and the ribbons and needles needed to catch the eye of an Indian lass, whether for a short-term or long-term relationship. When the kegs were empty, he rode off with a hangover for another lonely, vulnerable spring and fall in cold, fast-flowing streams, another winter staving off boredom in a sheltered valley, perhaps near the confluence of the Wind River and the Popo Agie.

No one became rich actually trapping. Ashley saw that the money was in financing and supplying; in 1826 he sold out to Smith, Jackson and Sublette. They sold out in 1830 to a group that included Bridger and Fitzpatrick, who in 1834 were forced to merge with the more powerful American Fur Company, which had established trading posts along the upper Missouri.

By 1840, beaver hats were out of fashion, and the Wyoming mountains were trapped out. Some mountain men returned to the States to farm, but others had the mountains in their blood and stayed. The one resource they had was intimate knowledge of a vast country that had hardly been mapped; this knowledge they put to use in a variety of ways.

Rendezvous

William Ashley further revolutionized the fur trade so that his men did not have to bring their furs to St. Louis or come east to resupply. Each spring he sent a pack train west with traps, powder, coffee, sugar and what was called whiskey—raw alcohol, to which ginger, molasses, or tobacco might be added for flavor—to a location decided

The Oregon Trail

In 1836 Eliza Spalding and Narcissa Whitman crossed South Pass, the first white women across the Divide. They and their husbands, who were being sent to the Columbia River Valley as missionaries to the Flatheads, traveled as far as the Green River Rendezvous with Fitzpatrick, who was leading the year's pack train. Eliza was shocked by Ren-dezvous, Narcissa delighted. Marcus Whitman, a physician, won the trappers' admiration by removing a Blackfeet arrowhead Bridger had carried in his shoulder for a few years.

Missionaries' reports from Oregon soon had middle-class families leaving eastern farms for the promise of a better life in the West. During the next two decades, thousands of

Wagon trains formed in Missouri for the trek west on the Oregon Trail. As parties followed the North Platte across eastern Wyoming, the country became higher, drier, stranger, more threatening. WILLIAM H. JACKSON WATER-COLOR; DENVER PUBLIC LIBRARY, WESTERN HISTORY DEPARTMENT

families, traveling with covered wagons that contained all they owned and were often pulled by cattle or oxen, followed the route the mountain men had pioneered. Some veteran mountain men found employment guiding emigrant parties.

Wagon trains typically formed in western Missouri. As they traveled overland to the Platte, started up the South Platte, and crossed to the North Platte, the country became increasingly strange, alarming, hostile—the grass sparser, the water alkaline, storms more violent, Indians more menacing. The size of the sky and the treeless prairie were themselves menacing. Animals weakened, and loads were lightened; the Oregon Trail was strewn with bones and furniture.

Fort Laramie in eastern Wyoming was an oasis, the first building in 600 miles; there the emigrants could resupply, repair, recuperate and get information.

The trail became wilder and more rugged beyond Fort Laramie. It continued up the North Platte to the Sweetwater, which it followed to South Pass. Fifteen or 20 miles a day was common on the prairie, but on the Sweetwater, emigrants, forced to lower wagons into gullies by rope and double-team oxen to haul the wagons up the other side, often had to be content with less than a mile in a day. Being caught by winter in the mountains, as the Donner-Reed party was in the Sierra in 1846-1847, was a source of constant anxiety. At Devil's Gate the Wind Rivers came in sight, and for several days they approached the seemingly unworldly snow dome of Wind River Peak.

Beyond South Pass, the original Oregon Trail followed Little Sandy Creek and the Big Sandy River down to the Green. As the country became better known, shorter variants were devised nearer the Wind Rivers' western flank, but streams and springs were far enough apart that a party had to hurry to get themselves and their animals to water by dark.

The various versions of the Oregon Trail met again at Fort Hall, near present-day Pocatello on the Snake River. At Fort Hall, however, the routes to Oregon and California diverged; a number of emigrants decided between Oregon and California at the last minute.

(continued on page 88)

The trail from Big Sandy Lake to the Cirque of the Towers crosses Jackass Pass, which in this view is hidden behind the foreground knoll, between Warbonnet (left) and Mitchell Peak (right).
JEFF GNASS

Albert Bierstadt

Colonel Frederick Lander had laid out an Oregon Trail "cut-off" that split from the original Trail near South Pass. Crossing the Little and Big Sandys nearer the base of the mountains, the Lander Cut-off eliminated the lengthy legs southwest to Fort Bridger and then back northwest to Fort Hall. After the Mountain Meadows Massacre in 1857 discouraged emigrants from traveling to California through Utah, Lander was sent west again, in 1859, to improve his road (ruts of which may still be seen near Buckskin Crossing, where a present dirt road crosses the Big Sandy), scout the rest of the route to California and placate Indians.

A young landscape painter, Albert Bierstadt, who had come to America from Germany, asked to accompany Lander's party. Near South Pass, Bierstadt left the surveyors and wandered around the southern end of the Wind Rivers, sketching the scenery. When Lander continued west, Bierstadt traveled only part way along the west side of the range, but after he returned east, his sketches evolved into vast oil paintings.

Bierstadt made a second trip west in 1863, in which he crossed Colorado and Utah to California, where he was captivated by Yosemite, then traveled north to Mt. Rainier. A third trip took the artist back to Yosemite again and to the High Sierra. A final western excursion, in 1881, had as its destination Yellowstone; his exact route is not known, but a painting entitled *En Route to Yellowstone* could represent the Wind Rivers.

Bierstadt's best-known painting, however, was a result of his first western trip. The enormous canvas, *The Rocky Mountains,* sold for what was then a record price for an American painting, $25,000, and now hangs in the Metropolitan Museum in New York.

The identity of the mountain that looms above the foreground Indian encampment has been a bit of a worry to scholars. An admiring contemporary critic stated that "an eminent American officer" could identify every feature of the painting. This officer is presumably Frémont, a friend and neighbor of Bierstadt, but no one since has been so successful at locating the peaks, ridges, falls, lakes and meadows. The focal peak also dominates other paintings, with such names as Sunset Light, Wind River Range of the Rocky Mountains, leaving no doubt as to the range that inspired the art. But the artist identified the peak in one of these paintings as "Frémont's Peak," which it does not look like. In another painting it was "Lander's Peak," which may have been a way of thanking his escort but which name is now attached to a less-conspicuous summit hidden in the heart of the range, to which neither Lander nor Bierstadt penetrated.

Bierstadt lurked around the southern Wind Rivers, which are dominated by Wind River Peak, and the featured peak is probably more Wind River

Peak—or what he and modern climbers wish it was—than anything else. However, if the main peak, which "leans" left and could harbor a steep cirque wall behind the left ridge, with a snow-capped peak behind, are reminiscent of an actual scene, it is the view from the west—from the Big Sandy—of Temple Peak with Wind River Peak as a high snow-capped summit peeking up behind.

We know that Bierstadt's most famous painting, "The Rocky Mountains," was based on the Wind Rivers. The identity of the scene or scenes that inspired the artist, however, is a matter of conjecture. It is possible to see the central peak as Temple and the snowy background summit as Wind River Peak, but, if so, much artistic license was involved, especially with the foreground. THE METROPOLITAN MUSEUM OF ART, ROGERS FUND, 1907. (07.123)

In this same painting the stream is the "Sweetwater," though not even Wind River Peak is visible from the Sweetwater until the river is well out in the plains. Adding to the disorientation is the drastic change of foreground from one painting to another. Completing the feeling of vertigo is the reappearance of *The Rocky Mountains'* waterfall and other foreground details in paintings of California. As a critic pointed out without even knowing the Wind Rivers, *The Rocky Mountains* is two paintings in one.

While locating Bierstadt's scenes makes a pedantic detective game, it is best to appreciate the paintings as how a 19th-century man, who had been trained in Europe and in the soft mists of the Hudson River valley, saw the West when it was a realm of overwhelming forces and scale that few eastern Americans had seen or expected to see. Bierstadt's Yosemite paintings, where the features are easily identifiable, provide an index of the artist's efforts at accuracy. He caught facets of El Capitan that only climbers would be expected to notice, indicating an eye for detail, but in a few fine paintings of the Cathedral Rocks, the two Cathedral Spires have migrated downhill to center stage from their secluded alcove and have lost their patient "Here we are" matter-of-fact posture for a sweep of line that begs the viewer to follow the craggy points up into the azure and beyond.

This combination of realistic detail improved with sublime fiction seems to be behind the features of Bierstadt's Big Sandy River. Warbonnet is recognizable near the right edge; below it lies Jackass Pass. Other Cirque towers are unimpressive from the vantage of the Big Sandy, being seen as talus slopes rising to a crest of gently rounded domes. However, in Bierstadt's rendition the ridge running from Warbonnet through the Warriors is transformed into a snow-mantled summit—not a snow peak that dominates the scene, as in *The Rocky Mountains,* but one of the painting's first features to catch the eye. Farther left, where the rubbly hulks of Pylon Peak and the Watchtowers should stand, is another distinct snow summit. Bierstadt has deepened the high, desolate indentation in the crest that separates the Warriors from Pylon to create a more distinct cleavage between his two snow peaks. To the left of the Pylon-Watchtower snow peak, however, stands a rock tower whose profile is that of Shark's Nose, which no artist could improve. To the left of the Cirque should be sky, but sticking out above the cottonwoods that line the river (and which migrated from far downstream, though they look as much like elms, which would have migrated a good deal farther) are castellated crags, which, if they really existed, would attract rockclimbers from afar and spare them the arduous backpack over Jackass Pass to the Cirque.

Above: *Mountain men have given way to mountain climbers, and the quest is not for beaver but for steep granite.* JOE KELSEY
Facing page: *Wind River Lake.* BRUCE SELYEM

South Pass City and nearby Atlantic City sprang up in 1868, as 5,000 people were attracted by the word "gold." Today the site of Atlantic City (seen here), a few miles from a highway, is nearly as peaceful as it was in 1867. BRUCE SELYEM PHOTOS

Gold rush

Rumors of gold at South Pass began in 1842 but went unconfirmed until 1867, when Mormons came upon a gold-rich vein. Gold rushes were easily precipitated in those days, and the name Clarissa Gulch caused a stampede. By the next summer two thousand men were tearing up the gulches and hillsides in search of a life of ease and status, and South Pass City was a county seat. Four miles to the east, Atlantic City sprang up, and four miles farther east, Miner's Delight.

Eventually, about 5,000 souls came to mine, but South Pass's quartz veins and placers never fulfilled their promise. By 1873, $2 million in gold had been extracted; by 1910, $5 million. Today South Pass is virtually deserted.

South Pass City has been restored by the state and is maintained as a low-key historical site.

An event took place in 1868 that, considering its significance, could not have occurred in a less likely place than South Pass. Esther Hobart Morris, a feisty citizen of South Pass City, gave a tea party—for the two local candidates for the territorial legislature. She made each promise that, if elected, he would introduce a measure giving women the right to vote. The winner, the Democrat Colonel Bright, kept his promise, and in 1869 Wyoming women became the first in America allowed to vote and hold office. In 1870, Ms. Morris became a justice of the peace—the world's first female J.P.

South Pass City once was the seat of Sweetwater County, which included present Frémont County. Today the state operates South Pass City as a historic site. CLOCKWISE FROM LEFT: BRUCE SELYEM, BRUCE SELYEM, GEORGE WUERTHNER, KENT AND DONNA DANNEN

Above: *A tributary of the North Popo Agie River.* GEORGE WUERTHNER
Facing page, left: *Mt. Geikie.* JOE KELSEY
Right: *Wolf's Head and Pingora.* DENNIS J. CWIDAK

The Hayden Survey

Americans still knew little about most of the interior West when the Civil War ended. By 1870, however, four government survey parties were filling in blank areas of the map. These surveys also studied, according to the interests of their leaders—Clarence King, John Wesley Powell, Lt. George M. Wheeler and Ferdinand Vandeveer Hayden—the geology, biology, archaeology, and ethnography of the regions they traveled through. With four teams covering domains that were ill-defined and with no central coordination—two were under the War Department, two under the Interior Department—the leaders often acted more like entrepreneurs than scientists, scrambling through Washington to protect their interests, increase their territories, increase their funding. Art was useful for attracting Congress's attention, and the surveys competed not only for turf but for the best artists—in particular, painter Thomas Moran, photographer William Henry Jackson and an unparalleled sketcher of topography and geology, William Henry Holmes.

The energetic Hayden, head of The Geological and Geographical Survey of the Territories, wandered unsystematically through Colorado and Wyoming, investigating what he found of interest. His investigations of the Yellowstone area, and Moran's subsequent paintings, had much to do with the creation of our first national park, in 1872.

The summer of 1877 found Hayden men in the Wind Rivers. A.D. Wilson led a survey party that left Camp Stambaugh, near South Pass, in late June. After climbing Wind River Peak and West Atlantic Peak from Sweetwater Gap, Wilson's party continued northwest, "keeping near the foot of the great granite plateau which here flanks the range." After passing "here and there some of those beautiful glacial lakes which lay imbedded between those great moraines," Wilson, with Ernest Ingersoll and Harry Yount, who had the important position with the Survey of hunter and later was Yellowstone Park's first ranger, "started for the point I then took to be Frémont's Peak." They set out early in the morning and reached the summit by 9 A.M., only to discover themselves on an insignificant peak west of the Divide; they report a latitude and longitude that fit the 11,857′ summit we call Mt. Baldy suspiciously well. Their consolation was a fine view of their intended objective, eight miles to the north, but the intervening country was covered so deeply with snow that Wilson postponed his assault on what was believed to be the highest peak in the range.

Another team, led by Frederick Endlich, left Camp Stambaugh to map the southern end of the range. Endlich and others made another ascent of Wind River Peak and also climbed Atlantic and Temple peaks.

Wilson was back in the Wind Rivers during the summer of 1878, later than in the previous year and with Jackson and Holmes along to depict the landscape. After another ascent of Wind River Peak, the surveyors headed north. This time they found their way to Frémont Peak, and on August 7 a group that included Wilson, Holmes, Jackson and Hayden climbed it. This was an era when glaciers were of much interest to scientists, and the surveyors were delighted to find glaciers on the north and east flanks of Wind River and Frémont peaks. Hayden reports them as the "first known to exist east of the Pacific coast."

To appreciate Jackson's photographic efforts, we must remember that he worked in an era when men were men and required a horse to carry their apparatus. With no prospect of getting even a mule up Frémont Peak, Jackson the evening before the climb coated plates "with colloido-bromide emulsion" and "dried them over a shovel." He developed his negatives upon returning from the climb, pronouncing them good except for "slight marks of the shovel."

While a Holmes sketch catches a triangulation team at work on the summit and behind them, according to Holmes's label, a "Snow capped peak north of Frémont's," Wilson's text gives no indication that the surveyors found this

peak to be higher than their present station. They were establishing a triangulation network across the West, and it was more important to sight lines to Wind River Peak and the Grand Teton than to an unknown nearby promontory. By the time the snow-capped peak was determined to be nearly 60′ higher than Frémont Peak, the four surveys had been consolidated as the United States Geological Survey, with first King, then Powell, as director.

The Chief Geographer of the USGS was Henry Gannett. Gannett, a Maine native and Harvard graduate, came to the Hayden Survey in 1872 in the position of "astronomer," having been given a qualified recommendation by a former teacher, California surveyor Charles Hoffman: "I do not recommend him as a draughtsman, but he can make a decent looking map and you will find him of great service in field work." Gannett was soon in charge of Hayden's survey parties, and remained with the Survey until its absorption into the USGS in 1879. Gannett was one of the founders of the National Geographic Society and was its president from 1910 until his death in 1914. A liking for statistics led to a prominent role in census-taking, and a desire to standardize geographic nomenclature led to the founding of the U.S. Board on Geographic Names. While these activities were eulogized by a friend as "skillful adaptation of the science of geography to the purposes of government," they also give the sense of a man given to organization and

Above: Gannett Peak, seen here from Mt. Woodrow Wilson, is most often climbed from the east (right) by way of Dinwoody and Gooseneck glaciers. JOE KELSEY
Facing page: While we may never identify the peak climbed by Bonneville, we can admire the setting, as the Captain did in 1833. He would have seen this view looking south from Mt. Chauvenet, which once was suggested as his summit. Wind River Peak, a more likely possibility, is the high skyline dome right of center, with East Temple and Temple peaks to its right. Near the right edge, the top of Lizard Head—once called Chauvenet—is barely visible. GEORGE WUERTHNER

detail, not the swashbuckling adventurer we imagine exploring the 19th-century West.

A "Dictionary of Altitudes" compiled by Gannett in 1884 lists Frémont Peak at 13,790' and the Grand Teton at 13,691' as the two highest Wyoming summits. A survey of 1905-1906 that led to the first topographic map of the area did however determine the eminence of the snowy peak as the highest in

the Rockies north of Long's Peak. Gannett—described as "painstaking, precise, ambitious"—was honored as Josiah Whitney, head of the California Geological Survey, and Sir George Everest, first Surveyor-General of India were—by having his name attached to a high point, so his name outlives any personal fame. Gannett did not climb his peak—indeed, it was not climbed until 1922—but he did make an early ascent of Mt. Whitney. Gannett was at work in Yellowstone when his colleagues were admiring the view from Frémont Peak.

The Hayden Surveyors, laboring in obscurity far from centers of science, were flattered at interest shown by eminent scientists. In 1877 Sir Joseph Dalton Hooker, botanist, president of the Royal Society, friend of Darwin and spokesman for evolution, an Englishman whose quests had taken him to Australia, New Zealand, Antarctica, the Himalayas and Tibet, joined the Hayden Surveyors to study the flora of the American West. Sir Archibald Geikie, director of the Geological Survey of the United Kingdom and author of several geology texts, wrote a glowing review of the Hayden maps in the journal *Nature*. The surveyors repaid these honors as well as they could: they bestowed the names of Geikie and Hooker on prominent Wind River summits.

It is apparent from the detail of their maps that Hayden Surveyors explored the range more thoroughly than the texts of their reports imply and saw more from the summits they visited than "making a few measurements" would indicate. They visited New Fork Lakes (though called by them Lac D'Amalia) as indicated by their knowledge that one lake is pluralized by a bisecting moraine—a visit confirmed by Jackson photographs. They apparently penetrated the East Fork Valley far enough to discover Pyramid Lake, for this secluded lake is visible from none of the summits they report visiting. If they did not ascend the Big Sandy River far enough to discover Big Sandy Lake's place as a hub collecting the drainage of several valleys, they must have studied the terrain below Wind River and Temple peaks more carefully than most modern climbers enjoying summit views. Dream, Raid and Cross lakes, below Mt. Bonneville, are recognizable by their shapes, even if they do lie among lakes not found on modern maps. With only a bit of imagination even Pingora and the East Ridge of Wolf's Head can be made out on one of Wilson's maps.

The maps also reveal a migration of a few names since 1878. The peak they named Bonneville we now call Raid, while Mt. Bonneville stands a mile to the north. The name Mt. Chauvenet drifted from our prominent Lizard Head Peak to an undistinguished rise on the plateau to the north. In 1878, Mt. Hooker stood on the Divide south of Haley Pass; today it stands on the Divide north of Haley Pass, while Dike Mountain has taken its place to the south.

WILDERNESS VALUES

Above: *A conflict in wilderness ethics near Soda Lake.* CHARLES W. KAY
Right: *Sunset at Bull Lake.*
SUNNIE F. LANCASTER
Facing page: *Climbers and hikers arriving in the Cirque of the Towers can expect to find clean campsites in any of numerous small meadows that are naturally secluded by boulders and clumps of trees.*
JEFF GNASS

The Wind Rivers are well traveled, considering the minimal law-enforcement in evidence. If the condition of the Wind River landscape is indicative of mankind's relation to his planet—when this relation is not confused with his relation to his government—the signs for humanity are mostly hopeful.

Last summer we passed a back-country ranger near Hobbs Lake—an unusual occurrence; the mountains are not heavily patrolled. We needed a break from heavy packs and soon were talking about humanity's effect on wilderness. I had recently camped by the creek that rolls, bounces and splashes down bedrock slabs from Deep Lake to Clear Lake. I had been annoyed that someone had tried to improve what I consider the Wind Rivers' prettiest stream by moving innumerable rocks to create diversion channels and dammed pools.

The ranger came back with her own complaint. "Okay," she said, "here's one for you. How about those stone wind breaks all over upper Titcomb Basin?" The rising tundra above Upper Titcomb Lake, at 11,000' and several miles from even a dwarf tree, can be windswept. As a convenient base for an ascent of Gannett Peak—and as a grassy valley set amid glaciers and thousand-foot walls—it hosts a dozen or more tents at a time during high summer. Some campers, in a futile effort to hold back the wind, have piled stones into walls perhaps two feet high and six feet long. It may be an application of Thoreau's observation that firewood warms you twice—once when you cut it and again when you burn it—except that with the stone walls, most of the warming must be in the piling. The ranger, seeing them as a sign of human intrusion, had scattered the stones, but with no conviction it was worth the trouble. I agreed: the windbreaks use native materials and are intended, at least, for an understandable purpose and left, presumably, for someone else's convenience. Yet they indicate humanity's irrepressible desire to "improve" wildness.

Such are the environmental issues we discuss in this barely spoiled landscape. It became fashionable during the early 1970s to make mankind feel guilty for setting foot in wilderness; any literature describing a wilderness was obliged to chastise people for intruding in it.

The Wind Rivers, however, more than most wilderness, make people feel at home. The thousands of acres of flowered meadows, the panoramic views, the streams and lakes and, by mountaineering standards, the human scale of the peaks—a person can feel that he or she belongs in the mountains. People feeling at home in the mountains are generally to be commended for their care in leaving it wilderness.

However, preservation is a matter of mystique, and the Wind Rivers are pervaded with more varied and richer mystiques than most landscapes. Climbers at faraway campfires, long before planning a trip of their own, hear the mystique in the inflection of storytellers. Mystique is a fragile entity, though, and various mystiques—some conflicting—whose balance has preserved the Wind Rivers could evaporate without being immediately missed.

On the one hand there is the sense of a Shangri La. In this sense the absence of authority aids the environment, because badges destroy the Shangri La effect. The Cirque of the Towers is kept much cleaner without law enforcement, without even the expectation of encountering authority, than well patrolled climbing bases in, say, the nearby Tetons. But there is also the "Wild West" mystique—the Wind Rivers as a last vestige of the Old West, where a man was free to do as he pleased.

The southern end of the range, south of wilderness boundaries, is a mess. A "road" of sorts—a dirt track—winds eight miles to Christina Lake. Every genre of vehicle imaginable—and some unimaginable, judging from isolated tracks taking short cuts—has traveled this road, been stuck in mud, experimented with alternate routes, especially across meadows. Roadside trash, when compared to the

Above: Golden trout, transplanted from California, thrive in several Wind River lakes and are the fish most sought by anglers. CHARLIE CRANGLE

Right: "Throwing a diamond hitch when the horse allows it," is how climber K.A. Henderson described his 1927 view of horse packing. COURTESY K.A. HENDERSON

Below: "A wild bronc tries to throw his load" in another 1927 Henderson photo. COURTESY K.A. HENDERSON

trashless trails to the Cirque of the Towers, illustrate that paradoxical inverse correlation between the effort required to carry out litter and people's unwillingness to do so. Christina Lake is what wilderness managers call a "sacrifice area"—a small fraction of the range where one sort of wilderness mystique can be concentrated.

Hikers complain about horses, especially when rain leaves trails muddy. Horses are a western tradition, and the trails were built for horses, but above treeline hoofprints easily damage tundra, and the tundra is slow to recover.

A few years ago climbers, who think of rock formations as immutable, were shocked to hear of a plan to tear apart Schiestler Peak, a few miles from the Cirque of the Towers, for its molybdenum, but the scheme turned out not to be economically feasible.

Currently the most controversial environmental issue is improvement of the Union Pass Road so that trucks can carry logs from Green River drainage to Dubois. On the one hand, Dubois is economically hurting and needs the logs, and wood must come from somewhere. On the other hand, past logging operations near Union Pass have shown no concern for environmental consequences and left the land in wretched condition.

But when wilderness preservation is discussed in the Wind Rivers, as when we met the ranger, talk inevitably turns to sheep grazing. Sheep, better able to live in dry country, better able to eat snow than cattle are, have for a century been wintered on the Red Desert to the south and driven to the high country on the west side of the Wind Rivers in summer.

Wool-growing, like mountaineering, has traditionally been done on America's frontiers. Sheepmen, like climbers, long have resented the imposition of government authority. Climbers, however, have two strong objections to sheep: their devastating effect on meadows, even if most meadows have survived a century of grazing, and the effect on solitude of a camp being overrun by hundreds of filthy, stupid beasts.

The Wilderness Act of 1964, which created Bridger Wilderness, among others, passed Congress with a compromise: that grazing, "where established," be allowed to continue "subject to such reasonable regulations as are deemed

necessary by the Secretary of Agriculture." Thus the Forest Service stands uneasily in the middle, mandated to manage the land for multiple uses. The Forest Service long has been subject to pressure from environmental groups and to pressure from livestock interests. One observer has pointed out that resulting Forest Service policy has tended to reflect the mood of America—tending toward environmental protection during the 1970s, favoring turning a profit from the land during the 1980s. But if recreational users are intimidated by sheepmen's claim of cost-effective use of the land, woolgrowers must be equally discomfited by hikers', climbers' and fishers' referral to spiritual values.

The Forest Service's multiple-use management has pleased neither side. Sheep people have seen the upper Big Sandy drainage, including the bowl below Jackass Pass and the valley of Deep Lake—country they found to be their best pasture—closed to grazing in deference to the heavy backpacking traffic. Backpackers are confronted with a host of signboards at Big Sandy Opening enumerating wilderness regulations—then head north to Fish Creek Meadows, Washakie Creek, or the East Fork Valley and find sheepherders ignoring the rules. Forest Service practice of not informing hikers where they will encounter sheep has not improved the situation.

Above: *Most of the Wind River Range is managed as National Forest Wilderness. The Forest Service does not preserve wilderness values by omnipresent back-country authority but instead posts rules at trailheads, such as on this signboard at Dickinson Park, and relies on the good will of visitors towards the land.* GEORGE WUERTHNER
Left: *The most-heated environmental controversy here at present involves logging near Union Pass.* ED WOLFF

River summits. Today the Uintas are visible perhaps once a summer, an event requiring a rare set of meteorological circumstances. For the past few decades, geologists needing long-range views have been resurrecting turn-of-the-century plates; blatant scratches are preferable to general haziness.

Recent concern with acid rain has intensified concern about air quality in the Wind Rivers and other ranges. Studies have found unacceptable levels of acidity in the range's highest lakes, far above treeline. This is of particular concern because these barren lakes lack the biological mechanisms that somewhat counteract acidity.

Some locals claim to be able to identify the source of western Wyoming air pollution according to its color: gray, brown or yellow. Let us say only that the prevailing jet stream brings air from the southwest and that it is polluted by a variety of sources, with other potential sources in the planning stage. So the environmental fate of the Wind Rivers is not only in the hands (or packs) of backpackers carrying out aluminum foil, orange peels, pop tops and gum wrappers, although each of us may like to believe that his or her snaring a windblown plastic bag or washing dishes away from a stream will somehow influence more global problems.

What the air brings to the Wind Rivers relates to our whole style of life. It is not enough to be environmentally conscious for a week or two during summer. Yet it is far less obvious how to be a good person for 52 weeks of the year.

Above: *Two traditional Wind River activities are grazing sheep in the high meadows and complaining about sheep in the high meadows. Both sheepherders and backpackers consider the land ideal for their respective activity, and the Forest Service is hard-pressed to set a policy that satisfies both factions.*
DENNIS J. CWIDAK

The one mitigating factor has been the decline of the markets for wool and lamb. Around 1900, as many as 130,000 sheep were run through the Wind Rivers in a summer. At present, the number is 10,000.

The acrimony of the conflict between recreational users and sheep can be attributed to its being immediate and local, with well defined "us" and "them." Unfortunately, some overgrazing and stream pollution may prove ephemeral compared to a more ominous threat, from the sky. As late as the 1960s, the Uinta Mountains, in Northeast Utah, were routinely visible on a clear day from Wind

Facing page: *From a camp at Island Lake, visible behind the foreground pond, John C. Frémont climbed the prominent peak by the ridge that here separates sun and shadow. The previous day Kit Carson had reached the summit of Jackson Peak (skyline, right edge) but was unable to cross the ridge connecting it to Frémont Peak.* CHARLIE CRANGLE

Wind River Peaks Above 12,000′

Forty-three Wind River summits are higher than 12,500′ and stand at least 500′ above any saddle joining them to a higher peak. They are:

Peak	Elevation	USGS Quadrangle	Peak	Elevation	USGS Quadrangle
Gannett	13,804	Gannett Peak	West Sentinel	12,585	Gannett Peak
Frémont	13,745	Frémont Peak S	North Cleft	12,548	Roberts' Mountain
Warren	13,722	Gannett Peak	Windy	12,539	Lizard Head Peak
Helen	13,620	Gannett Peak	Raid	12,532	Mt. Bonneville
Turret	13,600	Frémont Peak N	Unnamed	12,529	Frémont Peak S
Jackson	13,517	Frémont Peak S	Washakie	12,524	Mt. Bonneville
Woodrow Wilson	13,502	Gannett Peak	Hooker	12,504	Mt. Bonneville
Bastion	13,494	Gannett Peak			
Febbas	13,468	Frémont Peak N			
Flagstone	13,450	Gannett Peak			
Sunbeam	13,440	Frémont Peak N			
Downs'	13,349	Downs' Mountain			
Buchtel	13,205	Gannett Peak			
Unnamed	13,198	Frémont Peak S			
Wind River	13,192	Temple Peak			
Desolation	13,155	Gannett Peak			
Split	13,155	Gannett Peak			
Henderson	13,115	Gannett Peak			
Klondike	13,114	Gannett Peak			
Ellingwood	13,052	Frémont Peak S			
Bow	13,020	Gannett Peak			
Whitecap	13,020	Gannett Peak			
Knife Point	13,001	Frémont Peak S			
Temple	12,972	Temple Peak			
Three Brothers	12,960	Frémont Peak N			
Ladd	12,957	Gannett Peak			
Lizard Head	12,842	Lizard Head Peak			
Yukon	12,825	Downs' Mountain			
Roberts'	12,767	Roberts' Mountain			
Unnamed	12,730	Frémont Peak S			
Dry Creek Ridge	12,720	Frémont Peak N			
Wolverine	12,631	Roberts' Mountain			
Lander	12,623	Roberts' Mountain			
East Temple	12,600	Temple Peak			
Musembeah	12,593	Roberts' Mountain			
Bonneville	12,585	Mt. Bonneville			

Above: *Limber pine.* BILL RATCLIFFE

Facing page: *We like to picture the Wind Rivers as light, sunny mountains, but they are high mountains, and storms can develop quickly. Here clouds lower on Musembeah Peak.* JOE KELSEY

AMERICAN GEOGRAPHIC PUBLISHING

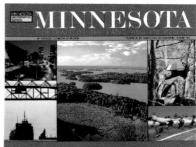

EACH BOOK HAS ABOUT 100 PAGES, 11" X 8 1/2", 120 TO 170 COLOR PHOTO-GRAPHS

Enjoy, See, Understand America State by State

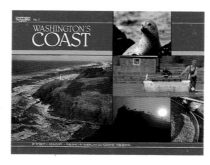

American Geographic Publishing
Geographic Series of the States

Lively, colorful, beautifully illustrated books specially written for these series explain land form, animals and plants, economy, lifestyle and history of each state or feature. Generous color photography brings each state to life and makes each book a treat to turn to frequently. The geographic series format is designed to give you more information than coffee-table photo books, yet so much more color photography than simple guide books.

Each book includes:
- Colorful maps
- Valuable descriptions and charts of features such as volcanoes and glaciers
- Up-to-date understanding of environmental problems where man and nature are in conflict
- References for additional reading, agencies and offices to contact for more information
- Special sections portraying people in their homes, at work, in the countryside

for more information write:
American Geographic Publishing
P.O. Box 5630
Helena, Montana 59604